H. Francke

Ladakhi Songs

First Series

H. Francke

Ladakhi Songs
First Series

ISBN/EAN: 9783337384746

Printed in Europe, USA, Canada, Australia, Japan

Cover: Foto ©Thomas Meinert / pixelio.de

More available books at **www.hansebooks.com**

LADAKHI SONGS.

EDITED IN CO-OPERATION WITH

Rev. S. RIBBACH and Dr. E. SHAWE,

BY

H. FRANCKE, LEH.

1899.

First Series..

INTRODUCTION.

When I wrote a paper on Ladakhi popular poetry about a year ago (published in Globus LXXV Nr. 15), my collection consisted of only 25 songs. Those songs had been collected in Leh, Stock and Sheh, that is, in the residences of the ancient Ladakhi kings and were all of the same type. As I had then been unable to discover any specimens of a more natural type of Ladakhi poetry, I concluded that really popular poetry was entirely absent in Ladakh. Meanwhile travels in Lower Ladakh and Purig, which extended my collection to about 150 pieces, have enabled me to discover other branches of Ladakhi poetry, which bear a less artificial character. I intend to publish them in little booklets of about ten songs each. Before issuing the first, I will in short describe the different types of Ladakhi poetry, as far as I have got to know them.

1. **The Court song.** It has been fully described in the Globus. Its principal characteristics are the following: The language is as near as possible to the book-language, a certain knowledge of Buddhism is displayed, it flatters persons in high position. It has no rhyme, but a certain rule of metre is strictly observed. The predominant metre is, that each line consists of three ~~dactyls~~. Specimens of the Court song we have in I, II, V and IX. The first line of I is pronounced thus:

tráshis phúnsumthsógspas.

In II it is pronounced

díchi gúngyi tsúgrgyan.

In consequence of the strict observance of this metric rule many of the sentences are incomplete, and the meaning can only be guessed from the context. It would be wrong to speak of compounds in all cases, when suffixes are missing. An analysis of a few sentences proves this.

2. **The Dance song.** Its language is the dialect of the country, where it is sung, religious ideas hardly ever come in; it tells in naive language the thoughts of people's hearts. It makes use of the rhyme of sentence, generally called parallelism, when occurring in European poetry. Two or more sentences are constructed accordingly, and in the corresponding places different words are inserted. Examples for illustrating this rhyme can be found in III, IV, VI, VII, VIII and X. These are two examples taken from IV.

6. *náchung gyávai yógkhorla rdzés,*
7. *Khyógthong gyávai skyédkhorla rdés,*

15. *gúnla rdzéspai gúndzes shig ín,*
16. *yángla rdzéspai yángdzes shig ín.*

In many cases the Ladakhi Dance song reminds us of Hebrew poetry; but as the principles of poetry in both countries are not the same, occasional conformities are more a matter of chance. Whilst the Ladakhi rhyme is, as many examples prove, a rhyme of sentence, the Hebrew form of poetry might be called a rhyme of thought.

The Dance song generally also has a metre, which is not of so strict a uniformity as that of the Court song. In it only the accentuated syllables are counted. The number of the unaccentuated syllables between them varies from one to three. As regards the accentuated syllables, the number 4 is predominant, but not of exclusive occurrence. Though IV is a Dance song in particular, all the other songs, mentioned above, (with the exception of III) may be sung at a dance. To show the exactness of the metric rule, examples may be given from the other songs also.

III. 1. *sámgul nang námgnl cóin léi,*
2. *jópa gár shégssed léi.*

Not observed in all verses, for instance not in 11, 12, 21.

VI. 1. 2. *thósai nang thónpo gun,*
námstod gun thólonpoi.

VII. *Khyérri yádo ngás mi shés,*
yádo Thséringskyid ngás mi shés,
mígsma gákhai náro még,
dágsa ína sólongséd.

X. *yúzhung dágse, máne sgángla bíngba.*

Because the number of the unaccentuated syllables is not limited, suffixes are hardly ever left out, and the sentences are complete.

Of the same form as the Dance song is the **song of the fairy tale**. In fairy tales direct speech is generally given in the form of a song.

3. **The Wedding song.** It is a kind of a catechism of the pre-buddhist religion of Ladakh. One verse contains many mythological questions, the next answers all of them. Its language is a more ancient form of the dialect, not the classical language. As it would not be good to separate single songs from the context, the Wedding songs will be published in a special booklet.

4. **The Drinking song** *(chang glu)*. It is of the same type as the Wedding song and of a very different character from what we should call a Drinking song. It may also be called a catechism of the pre-buddhist religion. At weddings it is the continuation of the Wedding song, but may be sung at many other feasts too.

Looking again at the first booklet of Ladakhi songs, we notice, that in IX the first letters of every line are arranged according to the order of the alphabet. In another song the first letters of the verses show the alphabet in inverted order. This form of poetry might have led to arranging the initials of the lines so as to represent a name, but I have not yet discovered such a song.

As regards the age of the popular poetry of Ladakh, I should not have entered into the question, but for Hanlon's having raised it in his paper (*Transactions of the 9th International Congress of Orientalists,* II., London, 1893). According to Hanlon the whole of the Ladakhi poetry is of modern origin, the oldest of the songs being about 100–200 years old. He comes to this conclusion, because several persons, mentioned in the songs, have actually lived 100–200 years ago. First of all, I think it necessary to state, that this method of fixing the age of a Ladakhi song, is not at all reliable. Just as the words of the national anthem 'God save the Queen' were originally 'God save the King,' the names, which Hanlon found in the Ladakhi songs, need not be those, which the poet had put in first. In some of them the names of the kings and ministers have been altered continually, until at present we find in them the present ex-king and ex-minister of Ladakh. If at the present time the power of the ex-king is praised in a song, it sounds like irony. As the Ladakhis are still very loyal to their old royal family, they would never think of composing ironical songs regarding it. Such songs can only be explained as having been handed down from ancient times and having been adapted to the present members of the once famous family.

But there are certain ideas occurring in some of the songs, which suggest a very high antiquity. That the wedding and drinking songs treat of the probably pre-buddhist religion of Ladakh, has already been mentioned. Another pre-buddhist idea we find in VI. The poet, who wrote VI, cannot have had an idea of the buddhist doctrine of re-birth. In fact the man, who taught me the poem, told me plainly, that now-a-days thoughts like those would not be spoken out. In another song, which treats of the seasons, only three seasons (autumn, summer and winter) are mentioned. Probably ancient Tibet, as many other countries, only knew of three seasons. I hope that later on in other booklets more proof of a very great antiquity of Ladakhi popular songs can be shown.

The orthography of the Ladakhi and Purig dialects has always kept as near to that of the book-language as possible.

As to the verb, the idea of the Ladakhis is, that its stem agrees fully with the perfect stem of the classical language, though in reality there are many exceptions. For this reason all the silent prefixed letters, which the classical perfect stem shows, are written with the Ladakhi verb, even when used for the present and future tenses. I thought I had better succumb to this general custom, and thus the orthography of these booklets is in accordance with the orthography of modern Ladakhi letterwriting.

I. THE KING'S GARDEN, LEH.

1. བཀྲ་ཤིས་ཕུན་སུམ་ཚོགས་པས།
2. བདེ་ལྡན་ཀར་བཟོའི་སྐྱེད་ཚལ།
3. མ་བཞེངས་ལྷུན་དུ་འགྲུབ་བྱུང་།
4. ཚངས་སྲས་ཉི་མའི་ཕོ་བྲང་།
5. གུང་གསལ་ནམ་མཁའི་ལྟོངས་ནས།
6. ཉི་ཟླའི་གདུགས་དང་ལྡན་བྱུང་།
7. ངོ་མཚར་དགའ་བའི་ལྟད་མོ།
8. གཟབ་ཁང་ཀ་བ་ཟུང་ལྡན།
9. ནང་ན་སེང་གེའི་ཁྲིའི་སྟེང་།
10. གཉའ་ཁྲི་བཙན་པོའི་གདུང་བརྒྱུད།
11. ཆོས་རྒྱལ་ཆེ་དཔལ་ཡུམ་སྲས།
12. ཞབས་པད་བསྐལ་བརྒྱ་བརྟན་ཤིག།
13. ལྗོན་ཤིང་སྟར་གའི་སྟེང་ན།
14. འདབ་ཆགས་ཕོ་མོའི་གསུངས་སྙན།
15. འོག་ན་སྟག་ཤར་འཛོམ་པོས།
16. བཀྲ་ཤིས་སྐྱིད་པའི་གླུ་ར་བྱུངས།

བསྟོད་ཚིགས་འདི་ཀར་བཟོའི་གཟབ་ཁང་ལ་སློལ་བློན་དངོས་གྲུབ
བསྟན་འཛིན་གྱིས་བྲིས་པའི་དགེ།

[2] *Karbzo* means "risen by itself" see dictionary *karlangba*, *skyedthsal* = principal garden, see also *skyedsgo*.

[4] *Thsangs sras*, holy sons, name of the gods (*lhas*).

[5] *Ltongs*, a high point (here zenith).

[10] *Gnyakhri*, Ladakhi for famous.

[13] *B. ljonshing*, the tree of paradise, any beautiful tree.

I. THE KING'S GARDEN, LEH.

1. Through perfect good fortune

2. The happiness containing garden *karbzo*

3. Not being built, was completed by itself.

4. It is the house of the gods and the sun.

5. Having in the zenith of the clear sky

6. Sun and moon like umbrellas, so it arose.

7. It is a wonderfully pleasing sight.

8. It is like a fine room with pairs of pillars.

9. Within on the lion's throne

10. Sits a famous and strong family.

11. That is *Chosrgyal Thsedpal* with mother and son.

12. May their lotus-like feet stand 100 kalpas !

13. On this magnificent high nut tree

14. Boys and girls sing melodious songs like birds.

15. Underneath the youths gather

16. And sing a song of happiness and welfare.

This song of praise was written by the Leh minister *dNgosgrub bstanadzin* in the fine castle within the *karbzo* garden.

[11] The King's name means 'religious king, glory of the time.'
[12] *Kalpa*, a fabulous period of time, at least 100,000 years. Skr.
[13] The royal family is compared with this high walnut tree, under whose shelter happiness dwells, walnut trees do not grow in Leh. 9 the lion's throne points to the King's castle, which was built in the middle of the garden.

II. THE ARISTOCRACY OF STOCK.

1. འདི་ཕྱི་ཀུན་གྱི་གཙུག་རྒྱན།
2. དྲིན་ཅན་ཙ་བའི་བླ་མ།
3. ནམ་ཀུན་ཐུགས་རྗེ་འགྱུར་མེད།
4. མཚུངས་མེད་དཔལ་ལྡན་འབྲུག་པ།
5. དགུང་སྔོན་མཁའ་ནས་ཤར་བྱུང་།
6. རྡོ་འཛམ་ཏྲ་བདུན་རྒྱལ་པོ།
7. མི་དབང་ཚོ་དཔལ་རྣམ་རྒྱལ།
8. འཛམ་གླིང་སྨུན་སེལ་སྒྲོན་མེ།
9. ཆོས་སྲིད་འཁོར་ལོ་བསྒྱུར་མཁས།
10. ལྷ་སྲས་ཚོ་དབང་རབ་བརྟན།
11. བསམ་འཕེལ་དབང་གི་རྒྱལ་པོ།
12. སྐྱེ་དགུའི་རེ་བ་བསྐང་བྱུང་།
13. ག་ཤུར་བསོལ་གཟེར་འཁྲོ་བའི།
14. ཉ་རྒྱས་ཟིལ་ཅན་མཁན་པོ།
15. ལྷ་ལྕམ་དཔལ་མཛེས་དབང་མོ།
16. ནམ་མཁའི་ཀུ་མུད་འབར་བྱུང་།
17. ལུགས་གཉིས་བརྒྱུད་ཚུའི་ཁྲིམས་སྐྱོང་།

1 *Gtsug rgyan*, amulet, worn on the head.
3 *Namgun* = *namsang*, always.
4 *Abruggpa*, name of one of the principal red sects.
8 *Adsamgling* = *adsambugling*.
16 *Kumud* = *Kumuda*, Lotus.

II. THE ARISTOCRACY OF STOCK.

1. The great protector (amulet) in this and in future life,

2. The lama, who is kind from the root,

3. He is of everlasting unchangeable mercy.

4. There is no equal to *dPaldan*, the red monk.

5. [Just as] out of the blue sky there rises

6. The warm and mild king (sun) with his seven horses,

7. So '*Mi dBang thsedpal rnamrgyal*' (the king)

8. Is the lamp, which illuminates "*adzambugling*."

9. Reigning religiously and turning the wheel wisely

10. Is the god's son '*Thsedbang rabbrtan*' (the king's brother),

11. The king of thoughtful power.

12. [In him] the hope of nine re-births is fulfilled.

13. Issuing cool beams like camphor

14. Is the bright full moon, so is the abbot.

15. The godly queen "*dPal mdzes dbangmo*"

16. Flourishes like a heavenly lotus.

17. She is the upholder of the 80 kinds of the two-fold custom.

[4] *dPalldan* means having glory.
[6] The Indian Haritas.
[7] The king's name means 'Lord of men, glorious time, king of all.'
[8] *Adzambugling* one of the Buddhist continents, about Asia.
[9] Turning the wheel of religion, Buddhist term for studying religion.
[10] The name means 'power of time, excellent firmness.'
[12] So people seem to understand this line; according to Jaeschke's dictionary the proper translation would be: the hope of many creatures is fulfilled.
[15] The name means 'beautiful glory.'
[17] Refers to the etiquette.

18. མངའ་འབངས་ཕན་བདེའི་སྐྱོང་མཁས།

19. དགུང་བློན་ཆེ་དབང་དོན་གྲུབ།

20. ལ་དྭགས་ཡོངས་ཀྱི་མཛེས་རྒྱན།

21. གོང་མ་བདག་པོའི་བཀའ་ལུང་།

22. ཅི་བསམ་དོན་བཞིན་འགྲུབ་བྱུང་།

23. ལྷག་བསམ་ཞལ་དྲིའི་འོད་དཀར།

24. ནང་སོ་དབང་གྲགས་དཔལ་རྒྱས།

25. ལྷ་དམག་འཛོམས་པོས་བཞེངས་པའི།

26. འཆི་མེད་ལྷའི་ཕོ་བྲང་།

27. ཏོག་མཁར་བཀྲ་ཤིས་གཡང་ཆགས།

28. ངོ་མཚར་ལྷུན་དུ་གྲུབ་བྱུང་།

29. མི་དབང་ཡབ་ཡུམ་སྲས་བཅས།

30. བསྐལ་བརྒྱར་ཞབས་པད་བརྟན་ཤིག།

31. ཆབ་སྲིད་ལོ་འདབ་རྒྱས་ཤིག།

32. ཕུན་ཚོགས་དབང་ཕྱུག་གི་སྨོན་ལམ།།

19 *Dgungblon*, respectful for *bkablon*, minister.
21 *Bkalung*, respectful for *lungbstan*, prophecy.
24 *Nangso*, he who takes care of the inside (of a house) the steward.
25 *Adsompos* = *adsompas*, having gathered.
27 *Tog*, ancient name of the village of Stock, means 'the top,' *chags* is originally a verb 'to produce,' here it must be taken as a substantive 'the producer,' 'the source.'
28 *Lhundu*, by itself.
31 *Chabsrid*, respectful for *srid*, government; *lo adab*, comp. cop. of *loma* and *adab*, means 'all leaves.'

18. The wise protector of the welfare of all subjects

19. Is the prime minister "*Thsedbang dongrub.*"

20. He is the joy of all Ladakh.

21. The prophecies of this high master,

22. Whatever he thinks, is fulfilled according to its meaning.

23. The white light of advice of superior thought

24. Is the castleward "*dBang grags dpal rgyas.*

25. The multitude of the god's having gathered built

26. The castle of the never dying gods,

27. The castle of Stock, the source of blessing and welfare.

28. It was completed in a wonderful way without man's work.

29. King *Mi dbang* and father, mother and child,

30. May your lotus-like feet stand 100 Kalpas!

31. May your reign grow like leaves (in spring).

32. That is '*Phuntshsog dbang phyug's*' prayer.

[19] The name means 'power of time, fulfiller of the aim.'
[24] The name means 'strong power, spreading glory.'
[29] Only the first part of the name is given, for full name see 7.
[32] The poet's name means, 'the perfect one, rich of power.'

III. THE GAME OF POLO.

1. ས་འགུལ་ནང་ནམ་འགུལ་ཅོ་ཡིན་ལེ།

2. ཇོ་པ་གར་ཤགས་སེད་ལེ།

3. ཡུལ་དཀྱིལ་ལི་ཤ་ག་རན་ལ།

4. ཇོ་པ་པོ་ལོ་ལ་ཤགས་སེད་ལེ།

5. ཅིག་དན་གྲོང་ངི་ཤ་ག་རན་ལ།

6. ཁན་པ་པོ་ལོ་ལ་ཤགས་སད་ལེ།

7. གྲེན་གྲེན་ནེ་གྲེན་པོ་ལ།

8. ཇོ་པས་གྲ་ཕོག་ཅིག་སལ་ལེད་ལེ།

9. ཐུར་ཐུར་རི་ཐུར་པོ་ལ།

10. ཇོ་པས་ཧལ་ཀ་རིག་སྲང་ངེད་ལེ།

11. དགའ་ཙ་ཁན་ཚོ་ཅིག་ཇོ་པས་འཐད་ཀྱུག་གིན་འགྲོང་ངེད་ལེ།

12. མི་དགའ་མཁན་ཚོ་ཅིག་པོ་ཇོ་པས་ཚོར་ཀྱུག་གིན་འགྲོང་ངེད་ལེ།

13. ཡར་རི་ཆིབས་ཆེན་པོའི་ཕྲོག་ལ།

14. ཇོ་ཡ་རང་ཡས་པའི་མེན་དོག།

15. ཡར་རི་ཆིབས་ཆེན་འོལ་ལ་ཉིང་དཀར་རི་ཕྲོག་ལ།

1 *Nang*, governs the accusative in Purig, and is used as a suffix of the Locative and instrumental.

2 *Shagsed*, present tense of *gshegspa*.

3 *Shagaran*, Purig for polo ground.

6 *Khanpa*, the ~~Persian Arabic~~ *Khan*.

8 *Graphog*, at the beginning of a new game one of the players throws the ball in the air in full gallop and hits it with the stick.

10 *Hal*, *halka*, goal, *srangnged*, present tense of *srongba*, pass straight through.

13 *Yarri*, contraction of *yarrangngi*, Purig for *nyerangngi*, your.

15 *Olla*=*olba*, black.

III. THE GAME OF POLO.

1. With an earthquake we shall shake the sky!
2. Where goes our Master?
3. To the Polo ground in the middle of the village.
4. There goes our Master for playing Polo.
5. To the Polo ground of the village *Cigtan*
6. There goes our *Khan* for playing Polo.
7. In the uppermost part (of the Polo ground)
8. Our Master hits the ball in the air.
9. In the downmost part (of the Polo ground)
10. Our Master hits it straight through the goal.
11. There our Master brings [the ball] to please his friends.
12. There the Master brings [the ball] to grieve the enemies.
13. There on your high horse
14. You are like a flower in bloom.
15. There on your high black horse with white hind feet

15 Horses are of different value according to their colour, those described in 15 are about the most valuable.

16. ཡར་རང་བཙོམ་པའི་ཆག་བྲུ།

17. ཨ་སྟ་ནང་ལ་གོང་ཡོག་གི།

18. ཡར་རང་སྐྱོམ་པའི་ཕ་ལི་ཡོད་ལེ།

19. འདིན་འདི་མདུན་བཟང་ཅན་པོ་ལ།

20. མིའི་ཁ་མོ་བཟང་པོ།

21. བཀའ་སློན་རའི་མཁན་ལ་ལོབ་སྟོང་ཚོ་སྨིན་ཞིག་ལེ།།

17 *Asta*, a certain part of the village (Purig).
18 *Skompa* in Purig has the meaning of protect.
19 *Adinadi* = *adiadi* = thus.
20 *Khamo* = fame.
21 *Lob stong* = 1000 years, in Purig *stong* seems to have a silent prefixed *b*.

IV. THE GOLDSMITH.

A Dance Song.

1st party. 1. གསེར་མགར་མཁས་པའི་གླུགས་ཕོར་པའི་ནང་ན།

2. གསེར་ནང་ར་གན་ཚང་ཅིག་ཡོད་ལེ།

3. གསེར་བོ་རྒྱལ་པོའི་ཁོག་ནོར་རིག་ཡིན་ལཻ།

4. ར་གན་ངན་པ་ཐང་ལ་སྐྱུར།

2nd party. 5. ཐང་ལ་མ་སྐྱུར་སྐྱིག་རེ་ཆེ་ལེ།

6. ན་ཚུང་བརྒྱ་བའི་ཡོག་ཁོར་ལ་བརྗེས།

7. ཁྲིག་ཐོང་བརྒྱ་བའི་སྐྱེད་ཁོར་ལ་བརྗེས།

2 *Nang*, within the gold there is brass, they are mixed.
3 *Rig* = *cig*, indefinite article.
4 *Re*, assumes here as sometimes in Purig the meaning of the indefinite article.

16. You are like a bunch of flowers.

17. Of the upper and lower part of the village

18. You are the protecting shield.

19. Thus before your excellent presence

20. There is a good rumour.

21. A lifetime of 1000 years may ripen for *Raim Khan* the minister.

IV. THE GOLDSMITH.

A Dance Song.

1st party. 1. In the melting pot of the clever goldsmith

2. There is gold and brass together.

3. The gold is the life-wealth of the king.

4. The bad brass throw on the plain!

2nd party. 5. Do not throw it on the plain, it would be a great sin.

6. Fasten it to the *yogkhor* of hundred girls.

7. Fasten it to the girdle of hundred [poor] youths.

[6] *Yogkhor* = lower wrappings, name of the sheep skin, which is worn over the shoulders, formerly it may have been wrapped round the waist.

1st party. 8. དངུལ་མགར་མཁས་པའི་བླུགས་པོར་པའི་ནང་ན།

9. དངུལ་ནང་རོ་ཉ་ཆང་ཅིག་ཡོད་ལེ།

10. དངུལ་པོ་རྒྱལ་པོའི་ཁོག་ནོར་རིག་ཡིན་ལེ།

11. རོ་ཉ་ངན་པ་ཐང་ལ་སྐྱུར།

2nd party. 12. ཐང་ལ་མ་སྐྱུར་སྡིག་རེ་ཆེ་ལེ།

13. ན་རྩང་བརྒྱ་པའི་ཡོག་ཁོར་ལ་བརྗེས།

14. ཁྲིག་ཐོང་བརྒྱ་པའི་སྐྱིད་ཁོར་ལ་བརྗེས།

15. ཀུན་ལ་བརྗེས་པའི་ཀུན་རྗེས་ཞིག་ཡིན།

16. ཡང་ལ་བརྗེས་པའི་ཡང་རྗེས་ཞིག་ཡིན།

V. THE ALCHI MONASTERY.

1. བདེ་སྐྱིད་ཕུན་སུམ་ཚོགས་པས།
2. བཟང་པོའི་རྟེན་འབྲེལ་འགྲིག་སོང་།
3. བླ་མའི་ཐུགས་ཀྱི་སྨོན་ལམ།
4. བཟང་པོའི་རྟེན་འབྲེལ་འགྲིག་སོང་།
5. སྣམ་ཞིང་ལོ་འདབས་རྒྱས་སོང་།
6. ཐུགས་ཀྱི་རྒྱ་མཚོ་ལེགས་གྲུང་།
7. བསྒྲུབ་ཐབས་གཞན་མོའི་དགོན་པ།
8. ལ་དྭགས་ཡོངས་ཀྱིས་ཆོས་སྐོར།
9. ཀ་གདུང་སེང་གེ་གཟེང་བསྒྲུབས།

1st party. 8. In the melting pot of the clever silversmith

9. There is silver and lead together.

10. Silver is the life-wealth of the king.

11. The bad lead throw on the plain.

2nd party. 12. Do not throw it on the plain! It would be a great sin!

13. Fasten it to the *yogkhor* of 100 [poor] girls!

14. Fasten it to the girdle of 100 [poor] youths!

15. It is a general ornament to be used by many,

16. It is a most general ornament to be used by many more.

V. THE ALCHI MONASTERY.

1. Through the most perfectly happy circumstances
2. The good auspices were fulfilled.
3. Through the prayers of the souls of the Lamas
4. The good auspices were fulfilled.
5. Green leaves came out of the dry wood.
6. Something good has happened on the ocean of souls.
7. The carefully built monastery is completed.
8. All Ladakhis may make the meritorious circumambulation.
9. With the chisel lion-like pillars were formed.

10. རི་མོ་ནོར་འཛིན་པ་ཏྲ།

11. ཞལ་ཆད་བརྟན་པོའི་ཆོས་སྐྱུང་།

12. མིང་གྲགས་རྡོ་རྗེ་ཆེན་མོ།

13. མིང་གྲགས་རྡོ་རྗེ་ཆེན་མོས།

14. ངསྟན་པ་ཡུལ་སྐྱུང་མཛོད་ཅིག།

15. ཡུལ་ངོས་ཡོངས་ཀྱི་གཟབ་མོའི།

16. བསྟན་པས་ཡུལ་སྐྱུང་མཛོད་ཅིག།

17. བྱང་ཆུབ་ཤིང་ལས་ཀོས་བསླུབས།

18. སྒོ་བསྒྲིགས་ཡོངས་ཀྱི་གཟབ་མོ།

19. གཡས་བཞུགས་གསེར་གྱི་སློན་པོ།

20. གཡོན་བཞུགས་ཡུམ་ནི་ལྷ་མཛེས།

21. སྐྱིལ་བཀྲུང་ས་དང་བསྐམས་བཞག།

22. ཤག་ཐུབ་བསྟན་པའི་ཉི་མ།

23. ཡུལ་ངོས་ཡོངས་ཀྱི་གཟབ་མོར།

24. རྡོ་རྗེ་གདན་གྱི་གནས་བཞུགས།

25. ཉི་མ་ཤར་ནས་ཕེབས་སོང་།

26. བླ་མའི་སློབ་མ་རྣམས་གཉིས།

27. དབུས་གཙང་གཞུང་ནས་ཕེབས་པས།

28. རྡུང་རམས་ཆོ་བརྟན་རྣམས་གཉིས།

10 *Patra*, originally 'begging bowl' Skr. is used for any religious receptacle, here book cases. *or is it patra?*

11 *Rdorje chenmo*, seems to be *phyagrdor*, one of the Ladakhi popular Boddhisattvas.

21 *Skyilbkrung*, a religious posture.

22 *Shagthub*, the powerful *shagkya*, comp. determ.

10. [Also] pictures and rich bookshelves.

11. The promise-keeping protector of religion

12. Is the famous great thunderbolt.

13. Oh, famous great thunderbolt,

14. Protect the teaching (religion) in the country!

15. Through a careful teaching in all directions

16. Protect the country!

17. From the wood of the holy fig tree ornaments were made.

18. The book cases more carefully than any other.

19. There on the right side sits the golden (rich) minister.

20. On the left sits mother *lHa mdzes*

21. On the plain ground with pious finger attitude.

22. The sun of the teaching of Buddha

23. Dwells better than in any other country,

24. On the place of the thunderbolt's throne.

25. From the east came

26. The disciple of the Lamas, the two-fold way

27. Arrived from the middle of *dBusgtsang*,

28. The doctor *Thsebrtan* [with the] two-fold way.

[19] The man who chiefly built the monastery.
[20] His wife.

29. རྣམས་གཉིས་མཐར་ཕྱིན་བསྒྲུབས་བྱུང་།

30. རྣམས་སྣང་གསེར་ལ་བསྒྲུབས་བྱུང་།

31. ཆོས་ཉིད་དད་པའི་ངང་ནས།

32. བཀའ་འགྱུར་བསྟན་འགྱུར་ཕེབས་བྱུང་།

33. གླུ་དབྱངས་རྒྱན་གྱིས་མ་རྫོགས།

34. བཀའ་འགྱུར་རིམ་གཉིས་བསྒྲུབས་བྱུང་།

35. ཨརྒྱི་དད་ལྡན་བྱུད་མེད།

36. བློ་སེམས་ཆོས་ལ་བསྒྲུབས་མཛོད།།

VI. PLEASURE OF YOUTH.

1. མཐོ་སའི་ནང་མཐོན་པོ་ཀུན།

2. གནམ་སྟོད་ཀུན་མཐོ་ལོན་པོ།

3. བྱ་རྒྱལ་མེན་ནེ་ལྡིངས་པ་རིག་མིན་འདུག།

4. དབྱར་ཟླ་གསུམ་གསུམ་ཅི་ཡས་ནའང་གང་ཡས།

5. དབྱར་ཟླ་གསུམ་མེན་ནེ་མེན་དོག་ལྷ་མེད།

6. མི་ཚེ་གཅིག་ཅིག་མེན་ནེ་བོ་མོ་ང་ཨ་མ་ལ་མེད་ལེ།

7. མི་ཚེ་གཅིག་ཅིག་པོ་ཅི་སྐྱིད་ནའང་གང་སྐྱིད་ལེ།

8. མི་ཚེ་གཅིག་ཅིག་པོ་ཅི་གཡངས་ནའང་གང་གཡངས་ཤིག།

[5] After *kun* a silent *nang*, corresponding to the first line must be supposed.

[6] *Menne*, lower Ladakhi for *mannas*, besides; *ldingspa* means originally to soar, *min adug*: the silent *a* of *adug* is sounded as a nasal, as is often the case.

[7] *Skyid* must here be taken for a verb as corresponding to *yangs*.

29. [Through] the two-fold way the salvation was fulfilled.

30. It was fulfilled to the golden *Dhyani Buddha.*

31. Out of (through) the great faith into religion itself

32. The holy scriptures and the commentaries have arrived.

33. With songs

34. The two unending ways of the scriptures are fulfilled.

35. Oh, thou believing *Alci*, unceasingly

36. Fulfill with heart and soul the religious teachings.

33 Because singing of religious songs is also considered to be meritorious.

VI. PLEASURE OF YOUTH.

1. The high ones (live) in high places.

2. Into all the heights of the sky

3. Besides the king of birds none flies.

4. During the three summer months, whatever can bloom, blooms.

5. Besides the three summer months, oh, there are no flowers.]

6. Besides this one life-time I shall not belong to my mother.

7. In this one life-time, whatever can be happy, is happy.

8. Enjoy this one life-time as ever you can enjoy it.

VII. THE BEAUTIFUL THSERINGSKYID.

First girl. 1. ང་རི་ཡ་དོ་མ་མཐོང་ས་ལྷ།
ཡ་དོ་ཚེ་རིང་སྐྱིད་མ་མཐོང་ས་ས།
Second girl. ཁྱེ་རི་ཡ་དོ་ངས་མི་ཤེས།
ཡ་དོ་ཚེ་རིང་སྐྱིད་ངས་མི་ཤེས།
སྒོ་བོངས་གསེར་ལ་བཞེངས་མཁན་མེག།
དགས་འདི་ན་སོ་ལོངས་སེད།།

First girl. 2. ང་རི་ཡ་དོ་མ་མཐོང་ས་ལྷ།
ཡ་དོ་ཚེ་རིང་སྐྱིད་ཨ་མཐོང་ས་ས།
Second girl. ཁྱེ་རི་ཡ་དོ་ངས་མི་ཤེས།
ཡ་དོ་ཚེ་རིང་སྐྱིད་ངས་མི་ཤེས།
སྤྲ་ལོ་གཡུ་བའི་རྒྱུ་ལྷུང་མེག།
དག་ས་འདི་ན་སོ་ལོངས་སེད།།

First girl. 3. ང་རི་ཡ་དོ་མ་མཐོང་ས་ལྷ།
ཨ་དོ་ཚེ་རིང་སྐྱིད་མ་མཐོང་ས་ས།
Second girl. ཁྱེ་རི་ཡ་དོ་ངས་མི་ཤེས།
ཡ་དོ་ཚེ་རིང་སྐྱིད་ངས་མི་ཤེས།
དཔལ་པ་བཙོ་ལྷའི་ཟླ་བ་མེག།
དག་ས་འདི་ན་སོ་ལོངས་སེད།།

[1] *Ngari* and *khyeri* are Lower Ladakhi abbreviations of *ngarangngi* and *khyedrangngi*; *sgobongs* = *sgobo*, body; *meg* = *ma ig* = *mashig*; *solongssed* = *songs sed* = *songste yod*, has gone, *lo* is inserted only for creating one more syllable.

VII. THE BEAUTIFUL THSERINGSKYID.

First girl. 1. Have you not seen my companion?

Have you not seen my companion *Thseringskyid?*

Second girl. Your companion I do not know,

Your companion *Thseringskyid* I do not know.

A girl, whose body was built as of gold

Was passing by here just now.

First girl. 2. Have you not seen my companion?

Have you not seen my companion *Thseringskyid?*

Second girl. Your companion I do not know,

Thseringskyid I do not know.

A girl with a mass of matted hair (full of) turquoises

Was passing by here just now.

First girl. 3. Have you not seen my companion?

Have you not seen my companion *Thseringskyid?*

Second girl. Your companion I do not know,

Thseringskyid I do not know.

A girl, glorious like the moon on the 15th

Was passing by here just now.

The whole is not to be taken seriously, the girls are teasing each other.

[3] On the fifteenth of the Tibetan month there ought to be full moon.

First girl. 4. ང་རི་ཡ་དོ་མ་མཐོང་ས་ལྦ།
ཡ་དོ་ཚོ་རིང་སྐྱིད་ཨ་མཐོང་ས་ས།

Second girl. ཁྲོ་རི་ཡ་དོ་ངས་མི་ཤེས།
ཡ་དོ་ཚོ་རིང་སྐྱིད་ངས་མི་ཤེས།
མིག་སྨ་ཀ་ཁའི་ན་རོ་མིག།
དགས་འདི་ན་སོ་ཡོངས་སེད།།

First girl. 5. ང་རི་ཡ་དོ་མ་མཐོང་ས་ས་ལྦ།
ཡ་དོ་ཚོ་རིང་སྐྱིད་ཨ་མཐོང་ས་ས།

Second girl. ཁྲོ་རི་ཡ་དོ་ངས་མི་ཤེས།
ཡ་དོ་ཚོ་རིང་སྐྱིད་ངས་མི་ཤེས།
སོ་ཞོ་ཧར་ནང་སྐུ་དྲིག་མིག།
དགས་འདི་ན་སོ་ཡོངས་སེད།།

First girl. 6. ང་རི་ཨ་དོ་མ་མཐོང་ས་ས་ལྦ།
ཡ་དོ་ཚོ་རིང་སྐྱིད་མ་མཐོང་ས་ས།

Second girl. ཁྲོ་རི་ཡ་དོ་ངས་མི་ཤེས།
ཨ་དོ་ཚོ་རིང་སྐྱིད་ངས་མི་ཤེས།
སྐྱིད་པ་རྡོ་རྗེ་དྲིལ་ལྷུ་མིག།
དགས་འདི་ན་སོ་ཡོངས་སེད།།

[4] *Migsma* = *aminma*, eye-brow.
[5] *Har* is either pearls of a rosary or as in Lower Ladakhi = white as if never used.
[6] *Rdorje drillu*, a bell dedicated to the Boddhisattva *phyagrdor*.

First girl. 4. Have you not seen my companion?

Have you not seen my companion *Thseringskyid?*

Second girl. Your companion I do not know,

Thseringskyid I do not know.

A girl with eyebrows like the *O* of the (Tibetan) alphabet

Was passing by here just now.

First girl. 5. Have you not seen my companion?

Have you not seen my companion *Thseringskyid?*

Second girl. Your companion I do not know,

Thseringskyid I do not know.

A girl with teeth like curdled milk and pearls

Was passing by here just now.

First girl. 6. Have you not seen my companion?

Have you not seen my companion *Thseringskyid?*

Second girl. Your companion I do not know,

Thseringskyid I do not know.

A girl with a waist like a monastery bell

Was passing by here just now.

First girl. 7. ང་རི་ཡ་རྡོ་མ་མཐྲོངས་ས་ལྷ།
ཡ་རྡོ་ཚེ་རིང་སྐྱིད་མ་མཐྲོངས་ས།

Second girl. ཁྲུ་རི་ཡ་རྡོ་ངས་མི་ཤེས།
ཡ་རྡོ་ཚེ་རིང་སྐྱིད་ངས་མི་ཤེས།
སི་ཀིམས་རྐྱང་ཤུད་སལ་མཁན་མེག།
དག་ས་འདི་ན་སོ་ལོངས་སེད།

Another person. 8. ཁྲོ་ཞ་ཚང་ཀ་ཤི་པི་རི།
ང་ཞིའི་ཁང་པ་ལ་ཅིལ་ཡོངས།།

[7] *Sikims* = silk from Sikim. *rkyangshud* = *rkyangskud*.
[8] *Shipi* the shoe-maker caste of Purig.

VIII. SECRET LOVE.

1. སྦྲང་ལ་སྦྲང་གོང་མ་སྦྲང་།
2. གོང་མ་སྦྲང་ལ་མེན་ཏོག་ཨས་སེད།
3. ལྷ་ཡ་རྡོ་པ།
4. གཟུགས་ཅན་ཡས་སེད་ལྷ་ཡ་རྡོ་པ།
5. མེན་ཏོག་སྦུས་ཤིག་ཡ་རྡོ་པ།
6. གཟུགས་ཅན་སྦུས་ཤིག་ཛ་མད་སག།
7. ལག་ནང་སྦུན་མེན་ཏོག་ལྡུད་པ་ཆེན།
8. སེམས་ནང་སྦུས་ཏེ་མེན་ཏོག་ཡིད་ལ་རྟོག་ལྷ།
9. སེམས་ནང་སྦུས་ཏེ་མེན་ཏོག་ཡིད་ལ་བོར།།

[6] *Jamadsag* is said to mean 'together,' 'gather together,' see X, note.
[7] *Ldudpa*, Lower Ladakhi for ruffled, faded.

First girl. 7. Have you not seen my companion?

Have you not seen my companion *Thseringskyid?*

Second girl. Your companion I do not know,

Thseringskyid I do not know.

A girl, who is spinning a silk thread,

Was passing by here just now.

Another person. 8. You all belong to the shoe-maker caste,

Why did you come to my house?

[8] This verse is either part of a different song, or it might be taken to express: Now we have had enough of this nonsense, go away!

VIII. SECRET LOVE.

The girl says: 1. On the meadow, on the upper meadow,

2. On the upper meadow there is a flower in bloom.

3. Hollah, my boy!

4. A flower of very fine shape is in bloom there, my fellow!

5. Gather the flower, my boy.

6. Gather the well-shaped flower!

7. If you gather it with your hand, it will fade.

8. Gather it with your soul and keep it (fasten it) in your mind!

9. Gather it with your soul and keep it in your mind!

IX. THE A B C SONG.

ཀ 1. བཀའ་དྲག་སེམས་ཀྱི་གནས་ལུགས།

ཁ 2. ཁ་ལྟར་དྲི་མེད་ཆོས་སྐུ།

ག 3. ག་ན་བལྟས་ཀྱང་མཛེས་བྱུང་།

ང 4. ང་ཡི་རང་སེམས་འདི་ཀ།

ཅ 5. ཅ་ཅོ་ཆོས་ལ་བསྒྱུར་ཀྱང་།

ཆ 6. ཆ་ལུགས་ཡིད་དང་མཐུན་པར།

ཇ 7. ཇ་ཆང་མཆོད་པ་མཆོད་གིན།

ཉ 8. ཉ་ར་སེམས་ལ་བརྗོད་དང་།

ཏ 9. ཏ་ལའི་ཐུགས་ཀྱི་འོད་གཟེར།

ཐ 10. མཐའ་མར་སེམས་ལ་འཕོག་ན།

ད 11. ད་ལྟ་ཡིད་ཀྱིས་རྟོགས་ན།

ན 12. ན་ཀ་འཆི་བ་མི་འདུག།

པ 13. དཔའ་བོ་ཤག་ཀྱ་ཆེན་པོ།

ཕ 14. ཕ་རོལ་ཉོན་མོངས་ཀག་ཉོན།

བ 15. བ་སླང་བཞིན་དུ་མ་ཉལ།

མ 16. མ་གཡེངས་དྲན་པ་སྐྱོང་ཞིག།

ཙ 17. ཙ་ཕྲན་བ་སྤྲུའི་བྲུ་ག།

ཚ 18. མཚན་ལྡན་བླ་མའི་དཀྱིལ་འཁོར།

ཛ 19. མཛའ་བོ་རང་སེམས་འདི་ཀ།

ཝ 20. ཝ་ལེའི་ངང་ལ་ཞོག་དང་།

[14] *Kagnon* in Lower Ladakhi means hinderer.

IX. THE A B C SONG.

1. The disposition of the teacher's soul
2. Is clean like snow, his transient body
3. Is beautiful, wherever you look at it.
4. This my own soul,
5. Though it agrees with religion as regards speech,
6. May my behaviour also agree with my mind!
7. When bringing the offerings of tea and beer,
8. Give that I may take care of my soul!
9. When the clear light of the Dalai Lama's spirit
10. Finally touches the soul,
11. All that at present I perceive in my soul,
12. Illness, old age, death, become nothing.
13. The great and powerful *Shakya*
14. Is the hinderer of misery in the other world.
15. Do not sleep like an ox,
16. Unchangingly, watch your soul!
17. [Fine] like a little artery or like a pore of perspiration
18. Is the doctrine of the famous Lama.
19. Friend! Also your own soul
20. Keep in clearness!

[9] This verse proves, that the name of Dalai Lama is not perfectly unknown to Ladakhis.

ཞ 21. ཞྭ་ལྷུར་རྟེན་པའི་བླ་མ།

ཟ 22. ཟག་མེད་མཆོད་པ་འབུལ་ན།

འ 23. འ་ལ་ཆོར་བའི་འདུ་ཤེས།

ཡ 24. ཡ་མཚན་སེམས་ཀྱི་ལྷུད་མོ།

ར 25. ར་རྭ་ལྷ་བུའི་སེམས་བརྒྱུད།

ལ 26. ལ་ཁུར་སྒྲུབ་པའི་དཔའ་བོ།

ཤ 27. ཤ་ཤད་སྐྱོལ་དུས་སྐོམས་མཛོད་དང་།

ས 28. ས་ལམ་སྒྱུར་དུ་སྒྲུབ་ཤིག།

ཧ 29. ཧ་ལ་རིག་པའི་རང་འགྲོལ།

ཨ 30. ཨ་མ་རྡོ་རྗེ་ཕག་མོ།

31. ཡུམ་ཆེན་ཁྲིད་དང་ང་གཉིས།

32. འདུ་འབྲལ་མེད་པར་ཤོག་ཅིག།།

23 *Ala* is an exclamation.
29 *Hala rig* is a name of *sPyanras gzigs.*

X. THE BRIDE'S FAREWELL.

1. གཡུ་ཞུང་བོ་བདག་སེ་སྨ་ནེ་སྒང་ལ་ཞིང་བ།
2. ཁྲུག་དཀར་པོ་བདག་སེ་སྨ་ནེ་སྒང་ལ་བཞིང་བ།
3. སྐྱེས་པའི་ཕ་མ་བསམས་སེ་ལོག་ཡིན་ལོག་ཡིན་བལྟས་ཕྱིན།
4. མཉམ་པའི་ཇ་མད་ཀུན་བསམས་སེ་ཕྱི་མིག་ལོག་སྟེ་བལྟས་ཕྱིན།།

1 *Se* = *ste*, gerundial termination in Purig; *maane*, a stone wall covered with stones bearing the inscription *Om maṇi padme hum.*
2 *Khrug* is perhaps a contraction of *Khrogyu.*
4 *Jamad* friends = *jamaad*, Hindustani for company.

21. When the Lama to whom I stick, as to my cap,

22. Brings a spotless offering,

23. Oh to have this sight (perception)

24. Is a wonderful spectacle for the soul,

25. Oh mankind, with hearts like the wind!

26. Oh, thou hero, who subduest even a pass-storm

27. Teach and at the same time explain (thy teaching)!

28. Fulfil quickly the path of perfection,

29. The Self-salvation of *sPyanras gzigs!*

30. Oh, mother *rDorje Phagmo*

31. Oh, great mother, thou and I,

32. May we without any separation always remain united!

29 The Boddhisattvas name means 'Sees with a clear eye.'
30 The mother's name means 'sow thunderbolt.'

X. THE BRIDE'S FAREWELL.

1. The turquoises being fastened, we arrived (came out) on the hill with the Manē.
2. The bright turquoises being fastened, we arrived on the hill with the Manē.
3. Father and mother, to whom I was born, thought I would come back, and I looked back.
4. The friends, with whom I was together, thought so, and I looked back.

XI. The three Seasons.

1. ཆགས་སེད་ལྷ་ཆགས་སེད་གསེར་མདོག་རིག་ཆགས་སེད་ལེ།

2. སྟོན་ནི་སྟོན་ཟླ་གསུམ་པོ་གསེར་མདོག་རིག་ཆགས།

3. ཆགས་སེད་ལྷ་ཆགས་སེད་གཡུ་མདོག་རིག་ཆགས་སེད་ལེ།

4. དབྱར་ནི་དབྱར་ཟླ་གསུམ་པོ་གཡུ་མདོག་རིག་ཆགས།

5. ཆགས་སེད་ལྷ་ཆགས་སེད་དུང་མདོག་རིག་ཆགས་སེད་ལེ།

6. དགུན་ནི་དགུན་ཟླ་གསུམ་པོ་དུང་མདོག་རིག་ཆགས།

7. དུང་མདོག་ཆགས་ན་ཡུལ་ཚུང་པ་ཙ་རི་འི་བསོད་བདེ།

Notes.

1. *Chagssed*, present tense of *Chagsces.*

XII. The Brahman Beggar.

1. ཤར་རི་ཁ་ཙུལ་གཞུང་ན་ཏམ་ཤ་ཡོད་ལེ།

ཨི་མོལ་ལེད་བྲམ་ཟེ་ལེ།

2. སལ་ལ་མེན་དོག་ཡང་འཛོན་ཏམ་ཤ་ཡོད་ལེ།

གང་མོལ་ལེད་བྲམ་ཟེ་ལེ།

3. ཤར་རི་ཁ་ཙུལ་གཞུང་ན་བྲས་དཀར་འོལ་ལོ་ཡོད་ལེ།

ཅི་མོལ་ལེད་བྲམ་ཟེ་ལེ།།

Notes.

= *shahr*, town, Hindust. *Tamàsha*, Hindustani for show, festival
n, a certain flower of Kashmir, which, people cannot tell.
kwhite, compare *'olgong* in "The Golden Boy".

XI. The three Seasons.

1. There grows, oh there grows, there grows a golden shade.

2. In autumn in the three months of autumn, there grows a golden shade.

3. There grows, oh there grows, there grows a turquoise shade.

4. During summer, during the three months of summer there grows a turquoise shade.

5. There grows, oh there grows, there grows a pearlwhite shade.

6. During winter, during the three months of winter, there grows a pearlwhite shade.

7. If it grows pearlwhite, it is for the welfare of the little village of *Pacari*.

Notes

3. If the green colour of vegetation in summer is compared with that of a Turquoise, it looks rather, as if the Ladakhis could not see a difference between green and blue. The idea is, that if in Winter much snow has fallen, the water for irrigating the fields will not run short.

XII. The Brahmin Beggar.

1. In the middle of the town of Kashmir there is a festival.

   What do you say [to that], oh Brahmin?

2. On the ground there is the festival of the *Yangdzin* flower!

   What do you say [to that], oh Brahmin?

3. In the town of Kashmir there is milkwhite rice!

   What do you say [to that], oh Brahmin?

Notes.

Brahmins, on their pilgrimage to the source of the Indus, often pass through Ladakh and ask alms from the people. The Ladakhis, who cannot understand the Brahmin's aims, ask, if they had not better stay in Kashmir, where there is so much better food and pleasure.

XIII. The Ibex.

1. ཨཏ་བའི་སྐྱིན་ནས་བའི་ཞང་ན།
2. སྐྱིན་ཆེན་བརྒྱ་དང་སྟོང་བསྡུས་སེད།
3. ལྷ་ཀླུ་ཀུནམ་འཐད་ན་སྲུ་འཐད་འདུག།
4. གཞི་བདག་ཀུནམ་འཐད་ན་སྲུ་འཐད་འདུག།
5. རུ་བ་ཁྱེར་རི་ཆོང་ལ་འདུག།
6. སྐྲ་ཁ་ཁྱེར་རི་གསེར་ལ་འདུག།
7. ཨཏ་བའི་དནས་བའི་ཞང་ན།
8. དནམོ་བརྒྱ་དང་སྟོང་བསྡུས་སེད།
9. ལྷ་ཀླུ་མེན་ནི་སྲུ་འཐད་འདུག།
10. གཞི་བདག་མེན་ནི་སྲུ་འཐད་འདུག།
11. རུ་བ་ཁྱེར་རི་ཆོང་ལ་འདུག།
12. སྐྲ་ཁ་ཁྱེར་རི་གསེར་ལ་འདུག།

Notes.

1. *ata*, father, in Lower Ladakh, Purig and Baltistan. 4. *gzhibdag*=owner of the ground, local deities. 5. *chong*, beads, made of carnelian stone. *khyerri*=*khyed—rangngi*, thine. 9. 10. *menne*= *mannas*, besides.

XIV. the Girl of Sheh.

1. རྒྱབ་རི་ཤེལ་དཀར་མཆོད་རྟེན།
2. མདུན་ན་གཡུ་མཚོ་སྔོན་མོ།
3. མཐའ་ན་མེ་ཏོག་འབར་བྱུང༌།
4. ཐ་ཡུལ་ཀྲིད་མཉམ་ཆགས།

XIII. The Ibex

1. In my father's place of (huntiug) the ibex
2. There gather hundreds and thousands of large ibex.
3. If the *lhas* and *klus* do not enjoy (this spectacle) who would enjoy it?
4. If the deities do not enjoy it, who would enjoy it?
5. The horns are thy carnelian ornament.
6. The colour of the hair is thy gold.
7. In my father's place of [hunting] the female ibex,
8. There gather hundreds and thousands of female ibex.
9. Besides the *lhas* and *klus*, who enjoys [this spectacle]?
10. Besides the deities, who enjoys [this spectacle]?
11. The horns are thy carnelian ornament.,
12. The colour of the hair is thy gold.

Notes.

3. *lha*, a god, *klu*, a waterspirit, prebuddhist deities. The meaning is that man hardly ever visits those regions and therefore cannot enjoy the spectacle. 5, 6, 11, 12 are addressed to the ibex. 11. Also the female ibex has small horns.

XIV. The Girl of Sheh.

1. On the hill in the back there is the *Chodrten* of white crystal.
2. In the front there is the lake, blue like a turquoise.
3. On the shore flowers are in bloom.
4. They grow in my fatherland together with its fortune.

མཐའ་ན་གསེར་ཆེན་འབར་བྱུང་།
ཞལ་མཁར་འོ་མ་འཁྱིལ་བྱུང་།
ཡ་སྟེང་རྩེ་ན་བཞུགས་པ།
རྩེ་བའི་རྩེ་ལྷ་སྐྱན་པོ།
བརྩེས་རྒྱལ་ཁྲུ་གར་སྐྱོད་ན།
ལྷ་ཡིས་སྐུ་སྲུང་མཛོད་དང་།
མི་དབང་སྲི་སྐྱོང་རྣམ་རྒྱལ་ལ།
ཚེའི་དངོས་གྲུབ་སྩོལ་དང་།
ནོ་མོས་མོས་པའི་བླ་མ།
ལྷ་ཁང་ལྷ་བྲིས་འདྲ།
བཟང་མོས་མོས་པའི་བླ་མ།
ལྷ་ཁང་ལྷ་བྲིས་འདྲ།
དམ་ཆོག་གཙང་མའི་ངང་དང་།
དཀོན་མཆོག་ལ་མཆོད་པ་འབུལ།
དམ་ཆོག་གཙང་མའི་ངང་དང་།
ངན་སློང་ལ་སྦྱིན་པ་དེང་།།

Notes.

This song was composed after the fashion of the courtsong, but the metre is not always strictly observed. 14. *lhabris* the written god, a picture of a god. 11. the name of the prince means 'power of men, protector of the nation, king of all.'

5. On the shore large yellow flowers are in bloom.
6. In the castle of Sheh the milk flows.
7. On the high summit there lives
8. The well speaking *lha* of the summit.
9. Wherever our gracious prince goes,
10. Oh *lha*, protect his life!
11. To *Midbang sdeskyong rnamrgyal*
12. Give blessing during his lifetime!
13. The Lama, who is loved by the girl
14. Is like a picture of the gods in the temple.
15. The Lama, who is loved by bZangmo
16. Is like a picture of the gods in the temple.
17. With pure and holy words
18. Bring offerings to God!
19. With pure and holy words
20. Give alms to the poor!

Notes.

1. *mchodrten,* a Ladakhi stupa. 2. there used to be a lake in front of the castle of Sheh. 6. milk a sign of abundance. 7. 8. Originally the *lhas* were supposed to live above the clouds and to descend only occasionally on certain hills, where little white altars were erected. Later on hilltops were believed to be the dwelling places of certain *lhas*. 13. 15. The girl who loves the Lama, is the poet of the song..

XV. Harvest festival at Skyurbuchan.

1. ཞག་ནང་སྐར་མ་འཛོམ་སེ་ཡོད།

མེན་དོག་ལྷན་མོ་ལེ།

2. སྐར་མ་རྒྱལ་སྤྱོད་ཤར་བའི་ཞག་ཡོད།

མེན་དོག་ལྷན་མོ་ལེ།

3. ཡར་ངོའི་ཚེ་ལྔ་གང་བའི་ཞག།

མེན་དོག་ལྷན་མོ་ལེ།

1st party. 4. མེན་དོག་ལྷན་མོ་གང་ནས་ཤགས།

མེན་དོག་ལྷན་མོ་ལེ།

2nd party. 5. མེན་དོག་ལྷན་མོ་ཤར་ནས་ཤགས།

མེན་དོག་ལྷན་མོ་ལེ །

I. 6. ཤར་རི་སྐད་ཚ་ཅེན་ད་འདུག།

མེན་དོག་ལྷན་མོ་ལེ།

II. 7. རྒྱལ་པོའི་དབུ་རྨོག་མཚོན་པོ་འདུག།

མེན་དོག་ལྷན་མོ་ལེ།

I. 8. མེན་དོག་ལྷན་མོ་གང་ནས་ཡོངས།

མེན་དོག་ལྷན་མོ་ལེ

II. 9. མེན་དོག་ལྷན་མོ་ལྷོ་ནས་ཡོངས།

མེ་དོག་ལྷན་མོ་ལེ།

XV. Harvest festival at Skyurbuchau.

This is the day of the constellation of the stars.

The flowershow, hurra!

2. It is the day of the finest of the lunar mansions.

the flowershow, hurra!

3. It is the 15 th, when the first half of the month is full.

The flowershow, hurra!

First party 4. From where do you bring these showy flowers?

The flowershow, hurra!

Sec. party 5. These showy flowers we bring from the East!

The flowershow, hurra!

I. 6. What news do you bring from the East?

The flowershow, hurra!

II. 7. There the kings helmet is very high!

The flowershow, hurra!

I. 8. From where do you bring these showy flowers?

The flowershow, hurra!

II. 9. These showy flowers we bring from the South!

The flowershow, hurra!

I. 10. ལྷོའི་སྐད་ཆ་ཅིན་ན་འདུག།

མེན་དོག་ལྷན་མོ་ལི།

II. 11. ལྷོ་ན་འབྲུ་སྣ་འཛོམ་མོ་འདུག། etc.

I. 12. མེན་དོག་ལྷན་མོ་གང་ནས་ཡོངས། etc.

II. 13. མེན་དོག་ལྷན་མོ་བྱང་ནས་ཡོངས། etc.

I. 14. བྱང་ངི་སྐད་ཆ་ཅིན་ན་འདུག། etc.

II. 15. བྱང་ན་ཚྭ་བལ་འཛོམ་མོ་འདུག། etc.

I. 16. མེན་དོག་ལྷན་མོ་གང་ནས་ཡོངས། etc.

II. 17. མེན་དོག་ལྷན་མོ་ནུ་བ་ནས་ཡོངས། etc.

I. 18. ནུབ་ཀྱི་སྐད་ཆ་ཅིན་ན་འདུག། etc.

II. 19. ནུབ་ན་ཚོས་སྣ་འཛོམ་མོ་འདུག། etc.

All. 20. ཤ་ཞང་པའི་མ་ཞིང་ལ་ལོ་ལགས་སེད། etc.

21. ཤ་ཞང་པའི་མ་ཞིང་ལྷང་འཁྲུངས་སེད། etc.

22. བརྒྱ་བང་གང་སྤྱི་སྤྱོང་བང་གང་། etc.

23. མེན་དོག་པ་མགྲོགས་ས་ལྷན་མོ་པ་མགྲོགས། etc.

24. དྲ་མན་པ་མགྲོགས་ས་ཆ་རིབ་པ་མགྲོགས། etc.

25. གངས་སྤྱོད་མཐོན་པོ་འི་སྤྱིང་ན། etc.

26. གངས་སི་སེང་གེ་གཡུ་རལ་ཅན་བཞུགས། etc.

27. སིང་ཕྲུག་ལེགས་མོ་འི་དགའ་བ་ལ་གཟིགས། etc.

28. བྲག་སྤྱོད་མཐོན་པོ་འི་སྤྱིང་ན། etc.

I. 10. What news do you bring from the South?

The flowershow, hurra!

II. 11. In the South there is abundance of all kinds of grain.

I. 12. From where do you bring these showy flowers! etc

II. 13. These showy flowers we bring from the North? etc.

I. 14. What news do you bring from the North? etc

II. 15. In the north there is abundance of salt and wool!

I. 16. From where do you bring these showy flowers?

II. 17. These showy flowers we bring from the West!

I. 18. What news do you bring from the West!

II. 19. In the West they dye with all kind of colours!

All. 20. From our uncle's motherfields there will be a good harvest!

21. In our uncles' motherfields the first green appears. etc.

22. The barns for 100 and 1000 bushels will be filled etc.

23. Hasten, you flowerboys, hasten, you dancers etc.

24. Hasten. you drummers, hasten you clarinet players etc.

25. On the top of the high icehill etc.

26. There sits the icelion with the turquoise mane etc.

27. Look at the joy of the lion's good child! etc.

28. On the top of the high rock etc.

29. སྨིན་ཆེན་བ་གན་བྲག་སྟེང་དུ་བཞུགས། etc.

30. ཤ་ཟླན་འཛོམ་མོའི་དགའ་བ་ལ་གཟིགས། etc.

31. མཁར་སྟོད་མཐོན་པོའི་རྩེང་ན། etc.

32. མི་ཆེན་གོང་མ་ཁྲིའི་ཁ་བཞུགས། etc.

33. གྲགས་ཞེན་འཛོམ་མོའི་དགའ་བ་ལ་གཟིགས། etc.

34. མ་ཁང་གྲུ་བཞིའི་ནང་དེ་ན། etc.

35. སྐྱིད་ཁང་གྲུ་བཞིའི་ནང་དེ་ན། etc.

36. ཡབ་ཡུམ་གཉིས་ཀ་བདེ་མོ་ནང་འདུག ། etc.

37. གཉེན་དྲུང་འཛོམ་མོའི་དགའ་བ་ལ་གཟིགས། etc.

38. ང་ཞ་ཚང་ཀའི་མེན་དོག་ལ་གཟིགས། etc.

39. ཕྲུ་གུ་པ་ཚང་ཀའི་མེན་དོག་ལ་གཟིགས།
མེ་ན་དོག་ལྷན་མོ་ལེ།།

Notes.

4. originally: from where does the flowershow come? 6. *rinda* ought to be spelled according to the views of Ladakhis *ri mda*, a parallel is *minda nyis, mi mda nyis*, about two men; thus a word mda [or perhaps *'ada*] 'about' seems to exist. 15. *adzommo* = *adzompo*, gathered, abundantly. 20. *pa* used as emphatic article, *lo lags sed*, it is a good year, the adjective is used as a verb. 23. *mgyogspa*, quick is also used as a verb. 26. *ralcan*, having locks of hair 34. *makhang*, motherroom, is a certain part of the house near the fireside. 39. *phrugupa*, the children as a body of dancers.

29. There sits the big ibex, the old ox. etc.

30. Look at the joy of all the young deer! etc.

31. There high up on the castle etc.

32. All the kings family is sitting on thrones etc.

33. Look at the joy of all the other famous men! etc.

34. Inside the fourcornered motherroom, etc.

35. Inside the fourcornered room of happiness etc.

36. Father and mother live in comfort, etc.

37. Look at the joy of all the assembled friends! etc.

38. Look at all our flowers! etc.

39. Look at the flowers of all the children!

The flowershow, hurra!

Notes.

The scene is the following: The village boys, who all summer long lived a shepherd life in distant secluded valleys, have to come down for the festival and dance whilst singing the above song; in their hands they carry long sticks covered all over with alpine flowers. In v. 4 — 19 we have a little play of answering questions, which almost exactly corresponds to wedding songs IV. The variations are the following: in the weddingsongs the abundance of colours is attributed to the North, and the West is considered famous for medicines. 20. motherfields are very fertile fields. 26. 27. The icelion and his child are originally the glacier and the brook, later on they developed into fabulous beings living there.

XVI A Dance.

1. སྒོ་བོངས་ནི་མོའི་གསེར་ལ་བཞངས་མཁན་ཡོད་ལེ།

2. སྣ་ལོ་ནི་མོའི་གཡུ་བའི་རྒྱལ་ལྷུང་ཡོད་ལེ།

3. གཡས་ལ་འཁོར་འདང་ཨ་མའི་བོ་མོ།

4. གཡོན་ལ་འཁོར་འདང་བསྐལ་བཟང་རོལ་མ།

5. རྒྱབ་དེ་ལ་ཆོག་འདང་ལེ།

6. རྒྱབ་རི་བཟང་པོ་ལ་ལྷ་སྡེ་རྒྱབ་དེ་ལ་ཆོག།

7. མདུན་དེ་ལ་བསྒུས་འདང་ལེ།

8. མདུན་ལ་བསྒུས་དེ་ཡར་ཁོ་དས་ལ་སེས་དར་ཚོས།

Notes.

1. *sgobongs* — *sgopo*, body. It is remarkable, that the genitive *nomoi*, is placed after the word it is related to. *lei* to be pronounced like Dutch *lij*. 4. *rolma* — *sgrolma*, see Ladakhi Gramm., laws of sound 8, the name means 'good *kalpa*, deliverer.' 5. *chog*, imperative of *gcogpa*, a sudden move backwards in a dance. 8. *khodus* — khuda, God, Hindustani. *xcedar* — sijdu, prayer, Hindustani.

XVII. Tobacco from Kashmir.

1. ཁ་ཟུལ་ཡིད་མག་པོ་ཧ་ཟར་རི་དམག།

2. སྐྱི་ཡིམ་ལ་སྣང་རྟོགས་འདང་མེད།

3. བུ་ཚོ་ང་རང་ཁ་ཟུལ་ལ་ཆ་ཟན།

4. སྨོམ་པ་ལ་སྨོམ་རྩ་རིག་ཡིན།

5. ཨ་ཡི་བུ་ཚོ་དབུས་གཙང་ལ་ཆ་ན།

XVI. A Dance.

1. The body of the girl is as if it was built of gold,

2. The hair of the girl is like a turquoise willow.

3. Now turn to the right, mother's daughter!

4. Now turn to the left, *Skalzang Rolma!*

5. Then break off backwards!

6. In the direction of the good hill in the back break off backwards!

7. Now again advance, meeting [your companion]!

8. Advancing again give honour to God on high!

Notes.

In this song we have a queer mixture of Buddhism and Mohamedanism. Whilst the word *khodas*, God, is only used by Mohamedan Tibetans, the name of the girl is quite a Buddhist one, also the idea of paying homage to god by an ordinary dance is perfectly Buddhist.

XVII. Tobacco from Kashmir.

1. Tobacco from Kashmir is the tobacco of lords.

2. There is no fear of its being filled into a general [pipe].

3. When I, a boy, shall go to Kashmere,

4. Then it will be water for the thirst.

5. When Ali, the boy, will go to Central Tibet,

6. ངལ་བ་རི་ངལ་འཚོ་རིག་ཡིན།

7. ཁ་རྒྱལ་ཡི་དམག་པོ་རྒྱ་ཡི་བའི་མེར་རྡོག།

8. སྤྱི་ལིམ་ལ་སྐྱང་རྡོགས་འང་མེད།

9. བུ་ཚང་རང་དབུས་གཙང་ལ་ཆ་ན།

10. སྨན་ན་སྨུན་རོགས་ཡིར་ལི།།

Notes.

1. *damag* — *thamakha*, tobacco; *hazar* — *huzur*. Hindust. 2. *spyilim* — *spyim*, compare First Series VII. *solongssed* — *songssed*. 6. *ngalbari*, in some villages, for instance Phyang, the genitive of the participle ends in *pari* instead of *mkhanni*; the verb *sunces* is used in Ladakhi mostly for 'being homesick.'

XVIII. Good Wishes to the Bridegroom.

1. ཞིག་བཟང་པོ་ལ་བལྟ་སྟེ།

2. ཨ་མའི་བུ་ཞུང་ངི་བག་སྟོན་བདང་ངེད་ལི།

3. སྐར་བཟང་པོ་ལ་བལྟ་སྟེ།

4. དངོས་གྲུབ་བསྟན་འཛིན་ནི་བག་སྟོན་བདང་ངེད་ལི།

5. ཨ་མ་ལ་བུ་ཞིག་སྐྱེ་ན།

6. ང་རི་བློན་ཆེན་ཚོགས་ཤིག་སྐྱེས་ཤིག།

7. སྟོངས་ཅན་རིག་སྐྱེ་ན་ལི

8. དངོས་གྲུབ་བསྟན་འཛིན་ཚོགས་ཤིག་སྐྱེས་ཤིག ||

Notes.

2. for *bushung* — *buchung* see Lad. Grammar, Kittel: laws of sound 6, the boy is not a very little one, the diminutive is only a sign of affection.
6. *ngari*, contraction of *ngaranggi*, our.

6. It will be like rest to the weary.

7. Tobacco from Kashmir is like apricot blossom.

8. There is no fear of its being filled into a general [pipe].

9. When I, a boy, will go to Central Tibet,

10. It will be my comforter, when I am homesick.

Notes.

2. this general pipe is the *hukka*, which is given round. 5. *Ali*, the boy, is the poet. The name is a Mohamedan one, the inhabitants of *Purig* being Mohamedans.

XVIII. Good Wishes to the Bridegroom.

1. Looking out for a good day,

2. We shall celebrate the wedding of mother's little son.

3. Looking out for a good star,

4. We shall celebrate the wedding of dNgosgrub bstan'adzin.

5. If a boy should be born to the mother,

6. A boy like our great minister be born!

7. If a clever boy should be born,

8. A boy like dNgosgrub bstan'adzin be born!

Notes.

1, and 3. refer to a good constellation of the stars. 6. the minister is the bridegroom himself.

XIX. Good Wishes to the Bride.

1. དམན་མཚར་མོ་ཉི་རང་བཟུམས་ཅན།

2. སྟང་ལྷ་ཡུལ་ལ་ཙང་ཞིག་བརྟུངས་སེད་ལེ།

3. དམན་མཚར་མོ་ཉི་རང་བཟུམས་ཅན།

4. གཡོག་ཀླུ་ཡུལ་ལ་དུང་ཅིག་རང་ཕྱུས།

5. དམན་མཚར་མོ་ཉིད་ཀྱི་པང་ལ་དཔལ་ལེ་ནང་སྲས་ཞིག་སྐྱེས་ལེ།

6. དམན་མཚར་མོ་ཉིད་ཀྱི་པང་ལ་དཔལ་ལེ་ནང་སྲས་ཞིག་སྐྱེས་ལེ།

7. ཕོད་རེ་རིག་སོང་ནང་ལེ།

8. གསེར་རི་ནང་གོ་ལུས་སལ་འདང་ལེ།

9. མ་ཕོད་པ་རིག་སོང་ནང་ལེ།

10. མཛེ་མོ་ནང་ཙུ་ཡོན་ཀུན་སལ་འདང་ལེ།

Notes.

2. *sed* = *ste yod*. 4. *kluyul*, the realm, not only of the watersnakes, but of the whole lower world.

5. *nang* is said to stand for *dang*, which in certain cases may be translated by 'like'. 7. *phodre* = *phodres* = *phodces*, parallel to *rig* = *cig*. 10. here the *nang* seems to have been added only for the sake of the met

XIX. Good Wishes to the Bride.

1. When you beautiful girl were born,

2. How many [drums] did they not beat then in heaven.

3. When you beautiful girl were born,

4. They blew on a shell in the underworld.

5. Oh beautiful woman, from your womb may be born a son like dPalle!

6. Oh, beautiful woman, from your womb may be born a son like d Palle!

7. If you should be able to do so,

8. Kindly give me a golden coat!

9. If you should not be able to do so,

10. Give me the crooked horns of a female Dzo!

Notes.

5. 6. *d palle* is one of the most famous heroes of the Kesarmyths. 10. although horns are often offered to the *lhas*, it is diffi cult to see, what the musician and singer wishes to do with them; people take this line for a joke.

XX. Preparations for a Dance.

1. གསོགས་བའི་ན་ཆུང་ཀུན་རྩེས་ལ་མཁས་པ།
2. རྩེས་ལ་བཞངས་འང་ན་ཆུང་ཚང་ཀ།
3. སྔོ་བོངས་བདེ་མོའི་འབོག་ཆུང་ཞིག་གོན།
4. ཤ་མདོག་བདེ་སོ་འི་ཤོག་ལོ་གསུམ་སྐུས།
5. འབོག་ཆུང་བོ་གོན་དེ་ལྷན་མོ་ལ་ཡོང་།
6. ཤོག་ལོ་གསུམ་བསྐུས་སེ་ལྷན་ཚོ་ལ་ཤོགས་འང༎

Notes.

4. shoglo, a herb, the yellow juice of which is smeared over the face.

ERRATA.

in the first series.

P. 12. note on 6, read *Mongol*, not *Persian Arabic*

P. 18. note on 10, read *Pātra*, not *Patra*; but probably the Tibetan word was derived from Skr. *pattra*, leaf, book.

XX. Preparations for a Dance.

1. The girls of the lower village are clever in dancing.

2. Get up then for a dance, all you girls!

3. To improve your figure, put on a shawl!

4. To improve your complexion, smear your face three times with *shogle*!

5. Having put on the shawl, come to the dance!

6. Having smeared your faces, come to the dance!

Scandinavian Alliance Mission Press,

GHOOM.

1900.

ཁ་ལ་ཙེའི་གླིང་གླུ་རྣམས་ཡིན།

XXI. Heavenly Voices.

1. ཨ་མའི་བུ་ཞིང་བསྐྱམས་པ་རི་དྭགས་ལ།
2. མི་ཡུལ་བོ་འོད་རིས་འང་ཁྲུངས།
3. ལྷ་ཡི་བུ་ཀེ་སར་ཀུན་བསྐྱམས་ཅན།
4. འཛོམ་བུ་གླིང་འོད་རིས་ཁྲུངས།
5. རྒྱལ་ལྷུང་ལྷུང་གི་ལྷུང་སྟོད་ན།
6. ལྷ་སྲུག་གསུམ་སྐྱོད་འདུག་ལོ།
7. ལྷ་སྐད་ཅིག་དི་རི་རི།
8. རྒྱལ་ལྷམ་ཆེན་མོ་ཀུན་སྐྱོད་ཅན།
9. ལྷ་སྐད་ཅིག་དི་རི་རི།
10. ལྷ་ཡི་བུ་ཀེ་སར་ཀུན་སྐྱོད་ཅན།
11. ལྷ་སྐད་ཅིག་དི་རི་རི།
12. རྒྱལ་ལྷུང་ལྷུང་གི་ལྷུང་སྟོད་ན།
13. ལྷ་མོ་ཀུན་སྐྱོད་དེད་ལོ།
14. ལྷ་སྐད་ཅིག་དི་རི་རི།
15. ཛེ་ཛོ་འབྲུ་གུ་མ་སྐྱོད་ཅན།
16. ལྷ་སྐད་ཅིག་དི་རི་རི།
17. ཞེལ་ལྷུམ་འབྲུ་གུ་མ་སྐྱོད་ཅན།
18. ལྷ་སྐད་ཅིག་དི་རི་རི།

These, songs, *i.e.*, Nos. XXI–XXIX are the *gling glu**of Khalatse.

XXI. Heavenly Voices.

1. When mother's little boy was born,
2. All the land of men was filled with light.
3. When Kesar and the [other] sons of the gods were born
4. All *'aDzambugling* was filled with light.
5. On the top of the willow of the world
6. There are walking three sons of the gods.
7. There is a hum of heavenly voices.
8. When all the great godly kings are walking
9. There is a hum of heavenly voices.
10. When Kesar and the [other] sons of the gods are walking,
11. There is a hum of heavenly voices.
12. On the top of the willow of the world
13. There are walking three goddesses.
14. There is a hum of heavenly voices.
15. When the noble *'aBruguma* is walking,
16. There is a hum of heavenly voices.
17. When *'aBruguma*, the crystal wife, is walking,
18. There is a hum of heavenly voices.

* *gLing glu* are those songs, which are sung at the time of the spring—or Kesar-festival, when everybody exercises himself at arrow-shooting.

Notes.

1. *bltamspari*, for participles ending in *pari* compare Song No. XVII Note on 6.—.2. 4. *khyangs;* just as *khyabpa* was derived from *'agebspa*, *khyangpa* was derived from *'agengspa*. 3 *kun*, for *kun*, in the sense of 'and so on' compare Kesarsage p. 33, note 19. 5. *rgyal lcang*, originally probably *rgya lcang*, the willow with far spreading [branches]. The prefixed *l* of the second syllable was sounded with the first. It is the tree of the world, mentioned in Ladakhi Wedding Ritual, songs Nos. V, VI, VII and VIII. 8. *rgyallham*, for the addition of final *m* see Kesarsage, p. 31, note V. 2. 13. *skyodded = skyoddad*, see Ladakhi Grammar, present tenses.

XXII. Dedication of Airows.

1. ཐང་ཀ་བདེ་མོའི་ཁ་མདའ་ཤིང་ལེགས་མོ་རིག་ཡོད།

2. ཐྲང་དེ་བདེ་མོའི་ཁ་མདའ་ཤིང་ལེགས་མོ་རིག་ཡོད།

3. མདའ་ཤིང་རིང་མོ་བོ།

ཨ་གུའི་མདའ་ཤིང་ཞིག་ཡིན་ལོ།

4. དེ་དྲུག་གི་མདའ་ཤིང་བོ།

ཨ་གུ་བའི་ལག་ཏུ་ཕུལ།

5. དེ་དྲུག་གི་མདའ་ཤིང་བོ།

ཨ་གུ་དྲུང་བ་བའི་ལག་ཏུ་ཕུལ་ལོ།

6. མདའ་ཤིང་ཆུང་ཆུང་བོ།

ཇོ་ཇོ་བའི་ཐང་ཤིང་རིག་ཡིན།

7. དེ་དྲུག་གི་ཐང་ཤིང་བོ།

ཨ་ནེ་ཡི་ལག་དེ་ལ་ཕུལ།

8. དེ་དྲུག་གི་ཐང་ཤིང་བོ།

ཨ་ནེ་བཀུར་དཀན་མོའི་ལག་དེ་ལ་ཕུལ་ལོ།

Notes.

If I am not altogether mistaken, this hymn contains an explanation of the phenomenon of the thunder. It is thought to be caused by the walking of the gods. The word *lhaskad*, which I translated by 'heavenly voices,' may be taken for any sound, caused by the mouths, hands or feet of the gods. The idea of the thunder is not so very far fetched, if we consider, that according to song No. XXIX, lightning is called 'Kesar's sword,' and that the word *diriri* may have been originally *ldiriri*, which is used to express the rolling of thunder.

XXII. Dedication of Arrows.

1. On the beautiful plain there is a fine arrow tree,

2. On that beautiful plain there is a fine arrow tree.

3. The long arrowstick

   is an arrowstick of the Agus.

4. Such arrowsticks

   offer to the hands of the Agus!

5. Such arrowsticks

   offer to the hands of those who are before the Agus!

6. The short arrowstick

   is a spindlestick of the ladies.

7. Such spindlesticks

   offer to the hands of the wife [of the heavenly king]!

8 Such spindlesticks

   offer to the hands of *Ane b Kurdmanmo!*

Notes.

5, 6, 7. the syllable *ba* in *agubai, drungbabai, jojobai* was inserted only for the sake of singing. 7. *jojo,* the reiterated form, is always used with the feminine, *jo* with the masculine.

XXIII. Kesar's Four Victories.

1. བྲུ་ཚ་ང་རང་ངི་དགུང་ལོ་བརྒྱད་པོའི་ནང་དུ།
ཤར་ཨན་དེ་བན་དྷེ་གསུམ་བཏུལ་བ་ཡིན།
བྲུ་ཚ་དེ་ཀུན་ནི་ཁ་འཁྱིང་འཁྱིང་རིག་འཁྱིངས་པ་ཡིན།

2. བྲུ་ཚ་ང་རང་ངི་དགུང་ལོ་བཅུ་གཉིས་པའི་ནང་དུ།
རི་རྒྱལ་སློན་ཆེན་ཀུན་བཏུལ་བ་ཡིན།
བྲུ་ཚ་དེ་ཀུན་ནི་ཁ་འཁྱིང་འཁྱིང་རིག་འཁྱིངས་པ་ཡིན།

3. བྲུ་ཚ་ང་རང་ངི་དགུང་ལོ་བཅུ་དྲུག་པའི་ནང་དུ།
བདུད་ཁྱབ་པ་ལག་རིང་ཀུན་བཏུལ་བ་ཡིན།
བྲུ་ཚ་དེ་ཀུན་ནི་ཁ་འཁྱིང་འཁྱིང་རིག་འཁྱིངས་པ་ཡིན།

4. བྲུ་ཚ་ང་རང་ངི་དགུང་ལོ་བཅོ་བརྒྱད་པའི་ནང་དུ།
ཧོར་ངན་ཀུན་བཏུལ་བ་ཡིན།
བྲུ་ཚ་དེ་ཀུན་ནི་ཁ་འཁྱིང་འཁྱིང་རིག་འཁྱིངས་པ་ཡིན།

Notes.

1. For the *Andebandhe's* of the East compare Kesarsage No. V, 1–8. There we have seven of them. 2. Kun, compare Note No. I, 3. 3. *Khyabpa lagring* means 'coverer longhand.' This is perhaps another name of Agu *Za* in Kesarsage No. III.

XXIV. Kesar and the Mules.

1. བྲུ་ཚ་ངའི་ངོས་ལ་ཉེན་དང་པྲ་དྲེ་ཞ་ཁས་པ།
2. བྲུ་ཚ་ངའི་བདག་ལ་གསན་དང་དྲེ་ཞ་ཁས་པ།

Notes.

All the arrows, used at the Kesar festival are to be considered as being dedicated, the longer ones to the Agus, the shorter ones to the heavenly queen *Ane bKurdmanmo.*

XXIII. Kesar's Four Victories.

1. When I, a boy, had reached my eighth year.

   I subdued the three Andebandhe's of the East.

   The boy has been triumphing over all of them.

2. When I, a boy, had reached my twelfth year

   I subdued all the great ministers of the hills.

   The boy has been triumphing over all of them.

3. When I, a boy, had reached my sixteenth year,

   I subdued the devil *Khyabpa lagring* and his men.

   The boy has been triumphing over all of them.

4. When I, a boy, had reached my eighteenth year,

   I subdued all the bad Yarkandis.

   The boy has been triumphing over all of them.

Notes.

In this song we have probably the four victories, which were prophesied in Kesarsage No. V. 11–16. Instead of the word 'Yarkandis' in 4 'Mongolians' may be said, compare Jäschke's dictionary.

XXIV. Kesar and the Mules.

1. Oh, you brown mules, listen to me, to a boy!

2. Oh, you brown mules, please, listen to me, to a boy!

3. རྩྭ་ཁ་ཞིང་གར་བཟང་པོ་ཟ་ཚོག་པ་འདུག།

4. དྲེ་ཞ་ཁམ་པ་ཁྲུང་ཁྲུང་བོ་ཅི་ལ་བཙོའད་ལེ།

5. ཚུ་མིག་གར་བཟང་པོ་འཐུང་ཚོག་ཅེས་འདུག།

6. དྲེ་ཞ་ཁམ་པ་ཁྲུང་ཁྲུང་བོ་ཅི་ལ་བཙོའད་ལེ།

7. ས་ལྗུབ་བདེ་མོའི་ཁ་འདུག་ཚོག་ཅེས་ཡོད།

8. དྲེ་ཞ་ཁམ་པ་ཁྲུང་ཁྲུང་བོ་ཅི་ལ་བཙོའད་ལེ།

Notes.

4, 6, 8. *Khung Khung* imitates the voice of the mules, *bo* is the emphatic article. 7. *saljub*, means the same as *sacha*, pasture ground.

XXV. On the Srar-Pass.

1. སྲར་གྱི་ལའི་སྟེང་ན་ཐང་དཀར་མགོ་དཀར་ཀུན་ཚད་དེ་ལུས་དེ་འདུག།
ཨ་ནེ་བཀུར་དམན་རྒྱལ་མོས་ང་ལ་རོགས་ཞིག་མཛོད།

2. སྲར་གྱི་ལའི་སྟེང་ན་ཕོ་རོག་ནག་ཆུང་ཀུན་ཚད་དེ་ལུས་དེ་འདུག།
ཨ་ནེ་བཀུར་དམན་རྒྱལ་མོས་ང་ལ་རོགས་ཞིག་མཛོད།

3. སྲར་གྱི་ལའི་སྟེང་ན་གསུ་མ་ཕོ་རོན་ཀུན་ཚད་དེ་ལུས་དེ་འདུག།
ཨ་ནེ་བཀུར་དམན་རྒྱལ་མོས་ང་ལ་རོགས་ཞིག་མཛོད།

4. སྲར་གྱི་ལའི་སྟེང་ན་ཤང་ཀུ་མཇུག་ཟླུམ་ཀུན་ཚད་དེ་ལུས་དེ་འདུག།
ཨ་ནེ་བཀུར་དམན་རྒྱལ་མོས་ང་ལ་རོགས་ཞིག་མཛོད།

5. སྲར་གྱི་ལའི་སྟེང་ན་སྲག་པ་ཙུན་དྲུ་ཀུན་ཚད་དེ་ལུས་དེ་འདུག།
ཨ་ནེ་བཀུར་དམན་རྒྱལ་མོས་ང་ལ་རོགས་ཞིག།མཛོད།།

3. There is quite enough of good pasture;

4. Oh, you brown mules, why are you making Khung Khung?

5. There is quite enough of good wells;

6. Oh you brown mules, why are you making Khung Khung?

7. You have been [long] enough on good pasture;

8. Oh, you brown mules, why are you making Khung Khung?

Notes.

This song is to be placed after Kesar's return from *Hor*. Then he found that the mules had taken the King of *Hor's* part. It is almost evident, that the word *'adre*, a certain spirit, was mixed up with the word *dre*, mule, and thus the original spirits became animals.

XXV. On the Srar-Pass.

1. On the *Srar*-pass the strength of the white-headed falcon is broken, and he remains back!

   Oh, queen *Ane bKurdmanmo*, come to my help!

2. On the *Srar*-pass the strength of all the little black crows is broken, and they remain back.

   Oh, queen *Ane bKurdmanmo*, come to my help!

3. On the *Srar*-pass the strength of all the turquoise pigeons is broken, and they remain back.

   Oh, queen *Ane bKurdmanmo*, come to my help!

4. On the *Srar*-pass the strength of all the bushy-tailed wolves is broken, and they remain back.

   Oh, queen *Ane bKurdmanmo*, come to my help!

5. On the *Srar*-pass the strength of all the earless stone-partridges is broken, and they remain back.

   Oh, queen *Ane bKurdmanmo*, come to my help!

chadde, in all the verses, means originally 'is cut off.' *rogs*=*grogs*, Lad. Gr. laws of sound 3. 3. *phoron*=*phugron*, pigeon. 4. *shangku*=*scangku*=*spyangku*, Lad. Gr. l. of. s. 1; 5, *cundru*, earless, derivation not known.

XXVI. Kesar, Returning to 'aBruguma.

1. གཡུ་མ་ཡོ་རོན་ལ་ཧྲུ་སྲེ།
གནམ་སྟོད་མཐོན་པོ་ལ་འཁྱིང་བ་ཆ་ན།
ཁྲ་སྐྱ་དཀར་པོ་ལ་ཧྲུ་སྲེ།
གཡུ་མ་ཡོ་རོན་ནི་སྣ་སྐྱིལ་ལ་ཆེན་ལི།

2. གཡུ་མ་ཡོ་རོན་ལ་ཧྲུ་སྲེ།
དགུང་སྟོད་མཐོན་པོ་ལ་ཕོར་ན།
ཁྲ་སྐྱ་དཀར་པོ་ལ་ཧྲུ་སྲེ།
གཡུ་མ་ཡོ་རོན་ལ་འདེད་པ་ཆེན་ལི།

3. ཉ་མོ་གསེར་མིག་ལ་ཧྲུ་སྲེ།
མཚོ་སྟོད་མཐྲན་པོ་ལ་འཁྱིང་བ་ཆ་ན།
ཆུ་སྲམ་ཀ་མ་ལ་ཧྲུ་སྲེ།
ཉ་མོ་གསེར་མིག་གི་སྣ་སྐྱིལ་ལ་ཆེན་ལི།

4 ཉ་མོ་གསེར་མིག་ལ་ཧྲུ་སྲེ།
མཚོ་རྒྱུན་མཐོན་པོ་ལ་ཕོར་ན།
ཆུ་སྲམ་བྲང་དཀར་ལ་ཧྲུ་སྲེ།
ཉ་མོ་གསེར་མིག་ལ་འདེད་ལ་ཆེན་ལི།།

Notes.

This song is a prayer rendered by Kesar, which he addressed to the queen of the gods, when crossing the difficult *Srar*-pass. This pass he had to cross on his journey to the North.

XXVI. Kesar, Returning to 'aBruguma.

1. If she, taking the shape of a turquoise dove,

Should go to soar in the highest skies,

I, taking the shape of a white falcon,

Will go to take her home again.

2. If she, taking the shape of a turquoise dove,

Should go to flee into the highest zenith,

I, taking the shape of a white falcon,

Will go to follow after her.

3. If she, taking the shape of the fish 'goldeye,'

Should go to float in the deepest ocean,

I, taking the shape of a whitebreasted otter,

Will go to take her home again.

4. If she, taking the shape of the fish 'goldeye,'

Should go to flee into the widest ocean,

I, taking the shape of a whitebreasted otter,

Will go to follow after her.

Notes.

1. *phoron*=*phugron*, dove; *sna skyil* literally 'hinder the nose,' *i.e.*, 'meet from the front.' 3. *Kama*, said to mean the same as *brang dkar*, whitebreasted. 4. *rgyan*=*rgya*, wide. Lad. Grammar, laws of sound 5.

XXVII. *'aBruguma's* Farewell to Kesar.

ཨེ་མ་ཁྲུལ་ལི་ཀེ་སར།

1. སྤངས་ཤན་ནི་རྒྱལ་པོ་ཉེ་རང་།
སྤིང་ནང་ལྷ་ཡུལ་ལ་སྐྱོད་ཟ་ན།
ལྷ་ཡུལ་ལི་ལྷ་མོ་ཀུན་མཐོང་སེ།
མི་ཡུལ་ལི་ཇོ་ཇོ་ཉིང་ཇེད་མ་ཇེད།།

2. སྤངས་ཤན་ནི་ཇོ་ཉེ་རང་།
སྙིང་ཉང་ལྷ་ཡུལ་ལ་སྐྱོད་ཟ་ན།
ལྷ་མོ་ནང་སི་དར་རྣམ་ཀུན་མཐོང་སེ།
མི་ཡུལ་ལི་འབྲུ་གུ་མ་འཕང་མ་འཕང་།།

3. སྤངས་ཤན་ནི་རྒྱལ་པོ་ཉེ་རང་།
ཡོག་ནང་ཀླུ་ཡུལ་ལ་སྐྱོད་ཟ་ན།
ཀླུ་ཡུལ་ལི་ཀླུ་མོ་ཀུན་མཐོང་སེ།
མི་ཡུལ་ལི་ཇོ་ཇོ་ཉིང་ཇེད་མ་ཇེད།

4. སྤངས་ཤན་ནི་ཇོ་ཉེ་རང་།
ཡོག་ནང་ཀླུ་ཡུལ་ལ་སྐྱོད་ཟ་ན།
ཀླུ་ཡུལ་ལི་ཀླུ་མོ་ཀུན་མཐོང་སེ།
མི་ཡུལ་ལི་གྲོགས་སྐལ་ཕང་མ་ཕང་།།

Notes.

Kesar, after having taken the food and drink of forgetfulness, had forgotten *'aBruguma*. Now, that the birds, coming from the South, brought him a message from her, decides to win her again by all means; actually there was no need to use the transformations, mentioned in the above song.

XXVII. *'aBruguma's* Farewell to Kesar.

Oh Kesar, who never lettest the fire fall!

1. Oh, my clever King!

When thou wilt go to the upper land of the gods,

And seest all the fairies of heaven,

Then do not forget thy wife from the land of men

2. Oh, my clever Lord!

When thou wilt go to the upper land of the gods,

And seest all the *Sitarrāms* among the fairies,

Then do not reject *'aBruguma* from the land of men.

3. Oh, my clever King!

When thou wilt go to the lower land of the snakes,

And seest all the *Nâgis* of it,

Then do not forget thy wife from the land of men!

4. Oh, my clever Lord!

When thou wilt go to the lower land of the snakes,

And seest all the *Nâgis* of it,

Then do not forget thy helpmate from the land of men

Notes.

1. *stangs shan* means 'clever in strategies; *zana*=*tsana*, when; *mthongse*=*mthongste*, seeing. 2. *sitarrām*, perhaps derived from Hindustani *sitár*, guitar; the *sitarrāms* may be heavenly musicians.

XXVIII. Young Kesar.

1. ལ་ཁྲ་ལ་ཡས་པ་བོ།

ལགས་མོ་བའི་མེན་དོག་ཅིག་ཡས་སེད་ལེ།

2. ཨ་སྟོད་ནང་མཐོན་པོ་ཀུན་ལ།

གཟུགས་ཤན་ནི་མེན་དོག་ཅིག་ཡས་སེད་ལེ།

3. ང་རྩུང་ཡས་པའི་སྐང་ཞིག་ཡོད་ལེ།

སྔ་མོ་ཡས་པའི་མེན་དོག་གི་ཇོ།

4. ང་རྩུང་ཡས་པའི་སྐང་ཞིག་ཡོད་ལེ།

ཀ་ལི་སྨན་ནི་མེན་དོག་གི་ཇོ།།

Notes.

3 and 4. may be translated just as well 'Oh Lord of the flower of the morning; oh Lord of the *Kalimān* flower.' The *Kalimān* flower is not of a beautiful appearance, but has a very fine smell.

XXIX. Kesar, the God of Lightning.

1. ས་རི་ཙན་ནི་ལ་མགོ་ན།

ནག་པོའི་སྤྲིན་ཅིག་ཡོང་ངེད་ལེ།

2. ས་རི་ཙན་ནི་ལ་མགོ་ན།

དུམ་དུམ་སྤྲིན་ཅིག་ཡོང་ངེད་ལེ།

Notes.

As the Kesarmyth tells us, Kesar forgot *'aBruguma* all the same, after having taken the food and drink of forgetfulness.

XXVIII. Young Kesar.

1. A flower, blooming on the pass,

Oh, a pure flower is in bloom!

2. On all the high passes

A flower of fine shape is in bloom!

3. Thou art but half opened,

Oh Lord [who art] like a flower of the morning!

4. Thou art but half opened,

Oh Lord [who art] like a *Kalimān* flower!

Notes.

This song refers to the supposed spring hero, who has carried spring up to the high passes. All the same he has not yet displayed his full glory, (the flower is only half opened).

XXIX. Kesar, the God of Lightning.

1. On the height of the *Sarican*-pass

Black clouds are gathering.

2. On the height of the *Sarican*-pass

Torn clouds are gathering.

3. ནག་པོ་སྨིན་པོའི་དཀྱིལ་དེ་ན།

ཇོ་ལགས་མོའི་སྣམ་རལ་ལ་གློག་འབར་རེད་ལི།

4. ནག་པོ་སྨྲིན་པོའི་དཀྱིལ་པོ་ན།

རྒྱལ་ལྷམ་ཀི་སར་རི་སྣམ་རལ་ལ་གློག་འབར་རེད་ལི།

Notes.

3, 4. *snamral*, respectful for *ralgri*, sword.

XXX. The Nyopa's Carpet.
A Wedding Song.

A. Nangmas :—

1. ནམ་སྟོད་མཐོན་པོ་དེ།

སྦུ་དང་གང་གི་སྟན།

2. གངས་སྟོད་མཐོན་པོ་དེ།

སྦུ་དང་གང་གི་སྟན།

3. བྲག་སྟོད་མཐོན་པོ་དེ།

སྦུ་དང་གང་གི་སྟན།

4. མཆིམ་སྟོད་མཐོན་པོ་དེ།

སྦུ་དང་གང་གི་སྟན།

5. ཨ་ཁར་སྟོད་མཐོན་པོ་དེ།

སྦུ་དང་གང་གི་སྟན།

6. ས་འོག་ཡོན་ཆེ་དེ།

སྦུ་དང་གང་གི་སྟན།

3. In the middle of the black clouds

   Lightning flashes from our good Lord's sword.

4. In the middle of the black clouds

   Lightning flashes from the godly King Kesar's sword.

Notes.

This song furnishes us with one of the strongest arguments to prove Kesar's nature-origin.

XXX. The Nyopa's Carpet.
A Wedding Song.

A. People of the house ask :—

1. The high sky,

   Whose and what carpet is it?

2. The high glacier,

   Whose and what carpet is it?

3. The high rock,

   Whose and what carpet is it?

4. The high ocean,

   Whose and what carpet is it?

5. The high castle,

   Whose and what carpet is it?

6. The wide earth,

   Whose and what carpet is it?

7. ཁྲོམ་ཟེད་ཁ་སྔོན་དེ།

སྲུ་དང་གང་གི་སྟན།

8. ཤ་སྟན་སེ་བོ་དེ།

སྲུ་དང་གང་གི་སྟན།

9. རྒྱ་ཤིང་ནགས་ཚལ་དེ།

སྲུ་དང་གང་གི་སྟན།

10. སྨན་བྲུ་ཡུག་རིང་དེ།

སྲུ་དང་གང་གི་སྟན།།

B. Nyopas :—

1. ནམ་ཕྱོད་མཐོན་པོ་དེ།

ཉི་ཟླ་གཉིས་ཀའི་སྟན།

2. གངས་སྤྱོད་མཐོན་པོ་དེ།

སེང་གེ་གཡུ་རལ་ཡི་སྟན།

3. བྲག་སྤྱོད་མཐོན་པོ་དེ།

སྤྲིན་ཆེན་བ་ཀན་ནི་སྟན།

4. མཚོས་སྤྱོད་མཐོན་པོ་དེ།

ཉ་མོ་གསེར་མིག་གི་སྟན།

5. མཁར་སྤྱོད་མཐོན་པོ་དེ།

མི་ཆེན་གོང་མའི་སྟན།

6. ས་འོག་ཕོལ་ཆེ་དེ།

ཀླུ་ནག་རྒྱལ་པོའི་སྟན།

7. The blue-bordered saddle-cloth,

   Whose and what carpet is it?

8. The grey deer-skin,

   Whose and what carpet is it?

9. Those meadows and woods,

   Whose and what carpet are they?

10. That long piece of woollen cloth,

    Whose and what carpet is it?

B. The Nyopas say:—

1. The high sky

   Is the carpet of sun and moon.

2. The high glacier

   Is the carpet of the lion with the turquoise mane.

3. The high rock

   Is the carpet of the mountain goat, the old ox.

4. The high ocean

   Is the carpet of the fish 'golden eye.'

5. The high castle

   Is the carpet of great men.

6. The wide earth

   Is the carpet of the King of China.

7. ཁྲོམ་ཟེད་ཁ་སྔོན་དེ།

ཨ་ཀུ་དཔལ་ལེའི་སྟན།

8. ཤ་སྟན་སེ་བོ་དེ།

ཨ་ཀུ་ཁྲུ་བཏུང་ངི་སྟན།

9. ཙུ་ཤིང་ནགས་ཚལ་དེ།

བྱ་དང་བྱི་གུའི་སྟན།

10. སྣམ་བུ་ཡུག་རིང་དེ།

ཉེའམ་སྲུན་བདུན་ནི་སྟན།།

Notes.

A. 4. *mthsom* = *mthso*, lake. 6. *phonche* or *pholche*, much, in this connection 'much land.' 7. *khrom zed* = *khromme zed*, 'glittering brush,' used for velvet. 10. *yug* means 'not sewn,' I am told ; thus 'a long woven piece of cloth.'

B. 3. *ba rgan*, old ox ; compare song No. XV. 29. 8. Agu *Khru btung* (the spelling of the name is doubtful) has not a human, but a falcon's head.

7. The blue-bordered saddle-cloth

Is the carpet of Agu *dPalle.*

8. The grey deer-skin

Is the carpet of Agu *Khru btung.*

9. Those meadows and woods

Are the carpet of the great and little birds.

10. That long piece of woollen cloth

Is the carpet of the *Nyopas,* the seven brethren.

Notes.

This song shows the general character of the wedding song very well. It is not in direct connection with the rest of the wedding songs, but forms a scene by itself. After the *Nyopas* (*lit.* "buyers" of the bride) have entered the house, they are not allowed to sit down on a carpet, until they have answered the questions, which form the first half of this song.

Meanwhile Dr. Laufer's criticism of my German paper on the Kesar-saga has reached me. In my English edition of the Kesar-saga which, I hope, will soon be published in the Indian Antiquary, I entered in full into his criticism. As regards the above songs, I can take up the responsibility as to the correctness of the Tibetan texts. The English translation is as literal as I could possibly render it without becoming unintelligible.

A. H. Francke.

XXXI. Preparations for the Bōno-nā festival.

Dard Text.

1. ཞག་་པོ་ནང་སྐར་་མ་འཛོམ་་པའི་ཞག་་།
2. སྐར་་མའི་རྒྱ་་སྟོད་ཤར་་པའི་ཞག་་།
3. མལ་་མལ་ལ་རྩ།
4. ད་་རྩ་ནེ་སང་ང་ཟིན་་ནེ།
5. ན་་རྩང་གྲལ་་ལེ་སང་ང་ཟིན་་ནེ།
6. ཚང་་རིགགི་ཚེན་་ནེ།
7. ཀན་་ཨ་རིའེན་་ནེ།
8. དུད་་ཨ་རིའེན་ནེ།
9. དོ་་དོ་འོ་་ཕྲུད་ཨ་རིའེནནེ།
10. ཕེ་ཕྲུད་ཨ་རིའེན་་ནེ།
11. མར་་ཕྲུད་ཨ་རིའེན་ནེ། པ་་ཧུ་ལེ་ས་་།
12. ཁོ་ལ་་དྲི་ཁོང་་མལ་ཨ་རིའེན་་ནེ།
13. ཕུ་་སྲོ་ཁནརྡི་ཡེན་་ནེ།
14. དུ་་དུ་ལེ།
15. མ་ཁྲི་རིང་་བྲག་བུ་མོ་ཨ་རིའེན་་ནེ།
16. ལ་ཁྲི་ལི་ལི་་ཡོ་པུ་་སྲོ་པ་་ཧུ་ལེ་ས་་།
17. ཚན་་དྲོར་ཕུ་་སྲོ་ཨ་རིའེན་ནེ།
18. པོ་དོ་ར་ཤ་་དཀྲ་ནུ་རྩ་ནུ་་།
19. ཨ་་དྲུའི་ཁོང་་ཡེའ་གས་ཨ་རིའེན་་ནེ།

XXXI. Preparations for the Bōno-nā festival.

Tibetan (Ladakhi) Translation.

1. ཞག་པོ་ནང་སྐར་མ་འཛོམ་པའི་ཞག།
2. སྐར་མ་ཞི་ཀྲུ་སྦྲོད་ཤར་བའི་ཞག།
3. ཅང་ར་ལ།
4. ཤར་པ་འཛོམས་ཤིག།
5. ན་ཆུང་བདེ་མོ་འཛོམ་ཤིག།
6. ཚང་རིགས་རྡོང་།
7. ཞོ་ཁྱོང་ཤིག།
8. འོ་མ་ཁྱོང་ཤིག།
9. དེ་ནས་འོ་ཐུད་ཁྱོང་ཤིག།
10. ཡེ་ཐུད་ཁྱོང་ཤིག།
11. མར་ཐུད་ཁྱོང་ཤིག། ར་ཧྲི་ཀུན།
12. ཁོ་ལག་དང་ཡེ་མར་ཁྱོང་ཤིག།
13. མེན་དོག་བདགས་ཤིག།
14. ཁ་རྒྱན་མེན་དོག།
15. ལྷ་ཙི་མེན་དོག་ཁྱོང་།
16. སྤང་རྒྱན་མེན་དོག་ཁྱོང་། ར་ཧྲི་ཀུན།
17. ཚན་དྲོར་མེན་དོག་ཁྱོང་།
18. དེན་ན་མ་ལ་ལ།
19. གུར་ཀུམ་མེན་དོག་ཁྱོང་ཤིག།

20. ཐོ་ནོ་དགུ་རྩགས་ཁན་དེའིན་ནེ།

21. ཡང་མ་དགུ་རྩགས་ཁན་དེའིན་ནེ།

22. ཀྲུ་ཡི་ནག་རང་ཁན་དེའིན་ནེ།

23. ཀྲུ་ཡི་སམས་བར་ཁན་དེའིན་ནེ།

24. ཀྲུ་ཡིཨས་ཤགཁན་དེའིན་ནེ།

25. འོད་དེ་ཨམ་བར་ཁན་དེའིན་ནེ།

26. ཧུང་ཧུང་ཀ་ནེ་མལ་ཁན་དེའིན་ནེ།

27. ལྷུ་བལ་མི་ཨིག་ཐ་ཕྲུ་ནེ་འན་ནེ།

28. ལྷུ་གུ་བལ་ཡི་ཙ་ཟར་ཕྲུ་ནེའིན་ནེ།

29. དེ་ཛའ་ནོ་མོ་ལེ་ཁོ་ད།

30. ནད་མེད་ཐེ་ཚི་རེ།

31. ལྷབ་བྲ་གི་ནེ།

32. ལྷ་དུས་ཚ།

33. མི་དུས་འཛོམ།

XXXII. Origin of the World.

Dard Text.

1. མི་ཡུལ་ནང་དང་པོ་ཡེ་ཞེ་ཆགས།

2. ཡར་ཀོ་མི་ཡུལ་མཚོ་ཞེ་ཆགས།

3. བའ་ཞེ་ཡེ་ཆགས།

4. བའ་ཞེ་པ་ཀུར་ཆགས།

20. ཆེན་མོ་དགུ་རྩིག་བཏགས་ཤིག།

21. དགས་འབར་མཁན་དགུ་རྩིག་བཏགས་ཤིག།

22. གུ་ལི་ནག་རང་གཏགས་ཤིག།

23. གུ་ལི་གུ་ལྷུབ་མེན་དོག་བཏགས་ཤིག།

24. གུ་ལི་རྐྱང་རྩིག་བཏགས་ཤིག།

25. ཨམ་བར་རི་མེན་དོག་བཏགས་ཤིག།

26. པོན་པོན་ཀ་ལི་སྣུན་མེན་དོག་བཏགས་ཤིག།

27. ལུག་གི་བལ་ལི་གོན་ཅེས་གོན་ཤིག།

28. ལུག་གུ་བལ་ལི་ཙ་དར་གོན་ཤིག།

29. ཉེ་རང་དཀོན་མཆོག་ལ་ཞུ།

30. ཐུག་མེད་དེ་བོར་ར་མཛད།

31. ལྷ་ལ་ཅོལ་ཞིག།

32. ལྷ་སྐུས་ཅོས་ཤིག།

33. མི་ཀུན་འཛོམ་ཤིག།

XXXII. Origin of the World.

Tibetan Translation.

1. མི་ཡུལ་དང་པོ་ཅིའི་ཁ་ལ་ཆགས།

2. དང་པོ་མི་ཡུལ་མཚོའི་ཁ་ཆགས།

3. ཆུ་ཡི་ཁ་ཅི་ཅི་རང་ཆགས།

4. ཆུ་ཡི་ཁ་སྤང་ཞིག་ཆགས།

5. པ་ཀུར་རི་ཞེ་ཡེ་ཚགས།

6. ཧུང་དེ་རྣ་ཚགས།

7. ཧུང་དེ་རྣ་ཟྣུ་ར་ཡེ་རཟ།

8. ཨེཀ་ཧུང་ངེ་ཟྣུ་ར་ཚོང་རི་ཕོ་ར་ཟི་སི་ནེ།

9. ཨེཀ་ཧུང་ངེ་ཟྣུ་ར་ཡེ་ར་ཟི་སི་ནེ།

10. ཨེཀ་ཧུང་ངེ་ཟྣུ་ར་ཚོང་རི་སྣོ་དོ་ར་ཟི་སི་ནེ།

11. ཨེཀ་ཧུང་ངེ་ཟྣུ་ར་ཡེ་ར་ཟི་སི་ནེ།

12. ཨེཀ་ཧུང་ངེ་ཟྣུ་ར་ཚོང་རི་ཉི་ལོ་ར་ཟི་སི་ནེ།

13. ཧུང་ངེ་དེ་ར་ཉིན་ཛེ་ཡེ་ཚགས།

14. ཀོ་དེ་དེ་རྣ་ཚགས།

15. དེ་རྣ་ཀོ་དོ་ཟྣུ་ར་ཡེ་ར་ཟི་སི་ནེ།

16. ཨེཀ་ཀོ་དོ་ཟྣུ་ར་ཙན་དན་ཕོ།

17. ཨེཀ་ཀོ་དོ་ཟྣུ་ར་ཙན་དན་ཉི་ལོ།

18. ཨེཀ་ཀོ་དོ་ཟྣུ་ར་ཙན་དན་སྣོ་དོར་ཟི་སིནེ།

19. དེ་རྣ་ཀོ་དོ་བུ་ཡེ་ཚགས།

20. དེ་རྣ་ཀོ་དོ་བུ་དེ་རྣ་ཚགས།

21. བུ་ཨེཀ་པོའི་ཟྣུ་ཧུ་ཡེ་ར་ཟི་སི་ནེ།

5. སྤྱང་པོའི་ཁ་ཅི་ཆགས།

6. སྤྱང་པོའི་ཁ་རི་གསུམ་ཆགས།

7. རི་གསུམ་པོའི་མིང་ལ་ཅི་ཞིག་རང་ཟེར།

8. གཅིག་པོའི་མིང་ལ་ཚོང་རི་དཀར་པོ་ཟེར།

9. རི་གཅིག་པོའི་མིང་ལ་ཅི་ཞིག་རང་ཟེར།

10. རི་གཅིག་པོའི་མིང་ལ་ཚོང་རི་དམར་པོ་ཟེར།

11. རི་གཅིག་པོའི་མིང་ལ་ཅི་ཞིག་རང་ཟེར།

12. རི་གཅིག་པོའི་མིང་ལ་ཚོང་རི་སྔོན་མོ་ཟེར།

13. རི་གསུམ་པོའི་ཁ་ལ་ཅི་ཞིག་རང་ཆགས།

14. ཤིང་གསུམ་ཆགས།

15. ཤིང་གསུམ་པོའི་མིང་ལ་ཅི་ཞིག་རང་ཟེར།

16. ཤིང་གཅིག་པོའི་མིང་ལ་ཙན་དན་དཀར་པོ་ཟེར།

17. ཤིང་གཅིག་པོའི་མིང་ལ་ཙན་དན་སྔོན་མོ་ཟེར།

18. ཤིང་གཅིག་པོའི་མིང་ལ་ཙན་དན་དམར་པོ་ཟེར།

19. ཤིང་གསུམ་པོའི་ཁ་ལ་བྱ་ཅི་ཞིག་ཆགས།

20. ཤིང་གསུམ་པོའི་ཁ་ལ་བྱ་གསུམ་ཆགས།

21. བྱ་གཅིག་པོའི་མིང་ལ་ཅི་ཞིག་རང་ཟེར།

22. བྲུ་ཤེག་པོའི་ཟྲྣུ་ར་བྲུ་རྒྱལ་གོད་པོ་ར་ཟྲི་སི་ནེ།

23. བྲུ་ཤེག་པོ་འི་ཟྲྣུ་ར་ཡེ་ར་ཟྲི་སི་ནེ།

24. བྲུ་ཤེག་པོ་འི་ཟྲྣུ་ར་ཀུར་ཀུར་རྫོལ་མོ་ར་ཟྲི་སིནེ།

25. བྲུ་ཤེག་པོ་འི་ཟྲྣུ་ར་ཡེ་ར་ཟྲི་སི་ནེ།

26. བྲུ་ཤེག་པོ་འི་ཟྲྣུ་ར་ཞེལ་ལི་གི་རྫོལ་མོ་ར་ཟྲི་སི་ནེ།

XXXIII. Hunting the Ibex.

Dard Text.

1. པོ་དོ་བྲུ་ཕལ་གི་ཡིད་དུ་ཙ་ནྡོ།

2. ད་ཙ་ནེ་ཕོ་ན་ཁྱིད།

3. ནང་གོང་ས་ཆོལ་ལུ་རེ་ནྡོ།

4. ནྲ་ཚུང་ཕོ་ན་ཁྱིད།

5. གི་ཡིད་དར་སྲུར་ཐེད།

6. གིལ་སེང་གེ་རྒྱལ་པོ་ཙེ་སེ་ཙོམ་མགོ་ཙ་ན་ཁྱིད།

7. པོ་དོན་ཚུང་ངས་ཡ་ཕ་གོ་དྲིག་ཐེ།

8. ད་ཙ་ནེ་ས་ཡ་ཕ་སྲུས་སིག་ཐེ།

9. ཡ་ཕ་དོ་དོ་དོ། ཚམ་མ་ཚྲམ་ཚྲམ།

10. ཨམ་བི་རི་ཨོན་དི་དརག་ཤེག་ཐེད་ལོ་ཀྲུམ་མོ།

11. ཕ་དོ་གོན་དོ་སླྲལ་ལོ་ཞལ་ལོ།

22. བུ་གཅིག་པོ་འདི་མིང་ལ་བུ་རྒྱལ་མཆོད་པོ་ཟེར།

23. བུ་གཅིག་པོ་འདི་མིང་ལ་ཅི་ཞིག་རང་ཟེར།

24. བུ་གཅིག་པོ་འདི་མིང་ལ་ཁྲིམས་བུ་ཟེར།

25. བུ་གཅིག་པོ་འདི་མིང་ལ་ཅི་ཞིག་རང་ཟེར།

26. བུ་གཅིག་པོ་འདི་མིང་ལ་ནག་པི་རྫུ་ཇོལ་མོ་ཟེར།

XXXIII. Hunting the Ibex.

Tibetan Translation.

1. དེ་ནས་བྲུ་ཤལ་གི་ཡིད་ལ་ཧེ།
2. ཀྱིག་ཕོང་བརྒྱ་ཡིང་སོང།
3. ར་ཤ་དྭགས་ཚོལ་ལ་ཧེ།
4. ན་ཚུང་བརྒྱ་ཡིང་སོང།
5. ཀི་ཡིད་ལ་མི་མང་པོ་འཛོམ་སོང།
6. གཡོལ་སེང་གེ་རྒྱལ་པོ་རྩེ་མཁན་གྱི་མགོ་ལ་ཡིང་སོང།
7. དེ་ནས་ན་ཚུང་ཚང་མས་ཡ་ཤ་ཁང་ལག་པ་ཁོར།
8. ཀྲོག་ཕོང་ཀུན་གྱིས་ཡ་ཤ་ཁྲུག་ཅིག།
9. ཡ་ཤ་ཧོ་ཧོ་ཧོ། ཚམ་མ་ཚམ་ཚམ།
10. རི་ཨེམ་ཡིར་ལ་རྡ་རག་ཅིག་ཟེར་སོང་བྲ་ཨ་ཞང།
11. གཉུ་དང་མདའ་དང་མདའ་ཡི་རིབུ།

12. རྫོག་ལེའག་ཤན་སུམ་མོ།

13. དཀར་པོ་འི་ཕེ་ཕུད་རྫོག་ལེའག་ཤན་སུམ་མོ།

14. དཀར་པོ་འི་མར་ཕུད་རྫོག་ལེའག་ཤན་སུས་མོ།

15. ཁོ་ལག་ཁོང་མར་རྫོག་ལེའག་ཤན་སུཡ་མོ།

16. རྟེ་བ་དོ་དོ་ཚེ་ལེའག་ཤན་སུས་མོ།

17. ཛོགས་པ་དོ་དོ་ཛོགས་ལེའག་ཤན་སུམ་མོ།

18. དིལ་དིལ་དོ་དོ་དིལ་ལེའག་ཤན་སུམ་མོ།

19. དོ་དོ་ཤ་ཀྲེ་ཀྲེ་ཕྱིའུང་། ཤ་རོ་རོག་རོག་རི་ཕྱིའུང་།

20. བྱོ་དོ་ཤ་གྲུ་ལོ་སུམ་མོ།

21. པོ་དོ་ཀོན་གྲུ་ལོ་སུམ་མོ།

22. དོ་སྐལ་ལོ་ཕལ་ལོ།

23. དྲག་དྲག་དོ་དོ་དྲག་ལེའག་ཤན་སུམ་མོ།

24. དོ་དོ་བུང་བུང་དོ་དོ་བུང་ལེའག་ཤན།

25. ཕལ་ཕལ་དོ་དོ་ཕལ་ལེའག་ཤན།

26. ཕྲང་ཕྲང་དོ་དོ་ཕྲང་ལེའག་ཤན།

27. ཕེ་ཕུད་མར་ཕུད་འོ་ཕུད་ཆུ་ཕུད།

28. པོ་དོ་བེ་ཕྲེ་ཆུན་ལོ་དིཛ་ནམོ་ལོ་ཁོདྲ།

29. བི་ཙག་ཏྲི་ཉི་ས་ཤལས་བྲི།

30. ཁ་སྒོ་བེ་ཕྲེ་ཆུན་སུམ་མོ།

12. ཡིབ་མཁན་གྱི་ཨ་ཞང་།

13. དཀར་པོ་འི་ཕེ་ཕྱུད་ཡིབ་མཁན་གྱི་ཨ་ཞང་།

14. དཀར་པོ་འི་མར་ཕྱུད་ཡིབ་མཁན་གྱི་ཨ་ཞང་།

15. ཁོ་ལག་ཁོང་མར་ཡིབ་མཁན་གྱི་ཨ་ཞང་།

16. རི་རྩེ་ལ་ཚ་ཅེས་ལ་མཁས་པའི་ཨ་ཞང་།

17. ཡ་ཟེར་དེ་སྒྲོགས་འང་ཨ་ཞང་།

18. དིལ་དིལ་སོང་སྔེ་མཐོང་ངེད་ལེ་ཨ་ཞང་།

19. དེ་ནས་སྤྲིན་ཀུན་རོག་རོག་མཐོང་ངེད་།

20. དེ་ནས་གཞུ་འཁོར་དེ་ཡོང་ལེ་ཨ་ཞང་།

21. དེ་ནས་མདའ་འཁོར་དེ་ཡོང་ལེ་ཨ་ཞང་།

22. མདའ་གཞུ་ལག་ཆ།

23. དྲག་དྲག་ཟེར་ཅེས་ཚོར་འདུག།

24. ད་ཕྲུང་ཕྲུང་མཐོང་ངེད་ལེ་ཨ་ཞང་།

25. ཕལ་ཕལ་ལ་འདུག་ལེ་ཨ་ཞང་།

26. ཁྲོ་རང་ཟེར་དེ་མདའ་བཏང་མཁན་གྱི་ཨ་ཞང་།

27. ཕེ་ཕྱུད་མར་ཕྱུད་འོ་ཕྱུད་ཚུ་ཕྱུད།

28. དེ་ནས་ལྷ་ལ་བསང་བཏང་ངེད་ལེ་ཨ་ཞང་།

29. ཕི་ཅག་རྟོན་པོ་དང་ཤའི་ནང་ན་ལམ་དོང་།

30. ཁ་སྒོ་མཆོད་པར་ཕྱུལ་ཡིན་ལེ་ཨ་ཞང་།

31. ཁམ་བུ་ར་ཁམ་ཞོ་རི་།

32. ད་ཙ་ན་ཤོ་འིན་དེ་ཨུ་ཟི་དྲི་དེ་ལོ་སྨུམ་མོ།

33. བོ་ཁར་སྨན་ཅེས་སྨུ་ཙ་ཁ་སྨྲོ་གྲུན་ལོ་སྨུམ་མོ།

34. པོ་དོ་ཨ་ཡེ་བོ་ཀྲུན་དེ་ཕུ་ལི་ཚུན་ལོ་སྨུམ་མོ།

35. ན་ཚུང་ང་ཤོ་འིན་དེ་སྨྲེས་གྲུན་ལོ་སྨུམ་མོ།

36. ཀྲ་མོ་སེན་མོ་ཅོན་ནུབ་པ་དེངས་ལོ་སྨུམ་མོ།

XXXIV. Dance of the Hunter.

Dard Text.

1. པོ་དོ་ཤ་རོ་སྲིང་ཀྱ་གྲུན་ལོ་སྨུམ་མོ།

2. ཨོན་ནེ་མདའ་གཉུ་ལག་ཆ་གྲུན་ལོ་སྨུམ་མོ།

3. ཤ་རོས་ཕྲུ་ཙ་གྲུན་ལོ་སྨུམ་མོ།

4. རྩེ་སི་རྩེམ་མགོ་ཙ་ཨུ་ཕེ་ལོ་སྨུམ་མོ།

5. རྩེས་ཚོད་དེ་བྲུས་གྲོད་དོ་ཤར་ཕྱོགས་སྨུ་ཙ་བྲུན་ལོ་སྨུས་མ།།

XXXV. Dance in Honor of the Yandring.

Dard Text.

1. ཧོ་ཡ་ཤ། ཡན་རྡིང། ཡན་རྡིང་བབ་པའོ་ཀྲུ་ནེ་བབས།

2. དོ་ལོ་ཧ་རང་ངེ་ཨུད།

3. ཧྨ་བྲིལ་བཟང་པོ་བེད་ལོ་སྨུམ་མོ།

31. ཁམ་བྲུ་ཁམ་ཅིག་དྲོང་།

32. ཏྲོག་ཕྲོང་བརྒྱ་ལ་ཁ་ལ་བདང་ཅེས་དྲོང་ལེ་ཡ་ཞང་།

33. ཐོལ་གར་སྨན་ཚས་ནང་ཁ་སྒྲོ་འཁྲུར་ཡིན་ལེ་ཡ་ཞང་།

34. དེ་ནས་ཨ་ཕ་དང་ཨ་མ་ལ་ཕྱུལ་ཡིན།

35. ན་ཚུང་བརྒྱ་ལ་སྐྱེས་འཁྲུར་ཡིན་ལེ་ཡ་ཞང་།

36. སྐྱིད་པོ་ནང་རྒྱུགས་པ་ལ་སླེབས་སོང་ལེ་ཡ་ཞང་།

XXXIV. Dance of the Hunter.

Tibetan Translation.

1. དེ་ནས་སྐྱིན་གྱི་རྭ་ཅོ་ཁྲུར་འང་ཡ་ཞང་།

2. གཡོན་པོ་ལ་མདའ་དང་གཞུ་ཁྲུར་འང་ཡ་ཞང་།

3. སྐྱིན་གྱི་ལྤགས་པོ་ཁྲུར་འང་ཡ་ཞང་།

4. རྒྱུ་སའི་མགོ་ལ་འཐོན་འང་ཡ་ཞང་།

5. རྗེས་ཟིན་ཚར་ན་ཤར་ཕྱོགས་ལ་རྒྱོད་ལེ་ཡ་ཞང་།

XXXV. Dance in Honor of the Yandring.

Tibetan Translation.

1. ཡུལ་གྱི་གཞི་བདག་ག་ནས་བབ།

2. གཙན་གྱི་དཀྱིལ་ནས་བབས།

8 རྟེན་འབྲེལ་བཟང་པོ་ཡིན་ནོག་ལེ་ཡ་ཞང་།

4. གོས་ཤེན་ཟར་བབ་སྲུ་ཉུན་ལོི་སྲུམ་མོ།

5. མག་མལ་ཨུ་གྲོད་ཕི་ལ་ཡུན་ལོི་སྲུམ་མོ།

6. དང་སེ་དོ་དོ་ལོི་དང་སེ་སྲུམ་མོ།

7. པོ་དོན་ཁྲི་ཟུན་ལོི་སྲུམ་མོ།།

XXXVI. Migrations of the Dards.

Dard Text.

1. པོ་དོ་དྲའི་རོང་ཚུར་རྒྱུད་དུ་ཙུ་ནུ་སླད་ལོི་སྲུམ་མོ།

2. རོང་ངེ་ཚུར་རྒྱུད་ས་ལི་ལོི་ཡ་ཤ་ཡན་རྡིང།

3. དང་སེ་དོ་དོ་ལོི་དང་སེ་མེན་ན་ཡན་རྡིང།

4. ཟ་ཤོ་གུ་སྲུར་ས་ལི།

5. གོ་ཨར་དོ་ཀུ་མར་ས་ལི་ཏོ་ཡ་ཤ་ཡན་རྡིང།

6. དང་སེ་དོ་དོ་ལོི་དང་སེ་མེན་ན་ཡན་རྡིང།

7. སྐར་རོ་གོར་རི་ལྷུང་ས་ལི་ཏོ་ཡ་ཤ་ཡན་རྡིང།

8. དང་སེ་དོ་དོ་ལོི་དང་སེ་མེན་ན་ཡན་རྡིང།

9. ཤི་གར་རི་ཆས་བྲོ་ཞིང་ས་ལི་ཏོ་ཡན་རྡིང།

10. དང་སེ་དོ་དོ་ལོི་དང་སེ་མེན་ན་ཡན་རྡིང།

11. ཀྲེ་རིས་ཚུམ་ཙགས་ལི་ཡན་རྡིང།

12. ཙ་སིང་མན་བྲོ་ཁར་ཤག་གལ་ས་ལི་ཏོ་ཡ་ཤ་ཡན་རྡིང།

4. གོས་ཕྱིན་ཟར་བླ་བ་གོན་ཡིན་ལེ་ཨ་ཞང།

5. མག་མལ་གྱི་ཁྲོད་བཅིང་ཡིན་ལེ་ཨ་ཞང།

6. འདི་བོ་གཡངས་པ་བདང་ས་མེན་ན་ལེ་ཨ་ཞང།

7. དེ་ནས་བིང་ཞིག་ལེ་ས་ཞང༎

XXXVI. Migrations of the Dards.

Tibetan Translation.

1. དེ་ནས་སོང་སྤེ་རོང་རྩ་རྒྱུད་ལ་བསྐྱིབས་སོང་ལེ་ཨ་ཞང།

2. རོང་རྩར་རྒྱུད་ལ་བསྐྱིབ། གཞི་བདག་ལ་ཡ་ཕ༎

3. འདི་བོ་ཡང་གཡངས་པ་བདང་ས་མེན་ན།

4. ག་སྲུར་ནི་བ་ཕོ་འཐོན་ས།

5. ཀོའུར་རྗེ་ཀོ་མར་ཡང་བ་ཕོ་འཐོན་ས། གཞི་བདག་ལ་ཡ་ཕ།

6. འདི་བོ་ཡང་གཡངས་པ་བདང་ས་མེན་ན། ཀྱི་གཞི་བདག།

7. སྐར་རྗེ་གོད་དི་ལྷུང་ར།

8. འདི་བོ་ཡང་གཡངས་པ་བདང་ས་མེན་ན། ཀྱི་གཞི་བདག།

9. ཕྱི་གར་གྱི་ས་ཁྲུད་ཀྱི་མིང་ལ་ཆམ་བྲོ་ཞིང་ཟེར་མཁན།

10. འདི་བོ་ཡང་གཡངས་པ་བདང་ས་མེན་ན། ཀྱི་གཞི་བདག།

11. ཀྱི་རིས་རྩམ་སྨག་དང།

12. ཤ་སིང་སྨན་བྲོ་མཁར་ཕྱག་ས་རྡན་གྱི་ས་ཁྲུད་ཏིག་ཞུག།

13. ཕར་ཀུན་ད་ནམ་ཀྱིལ་ས་ལི་ཧོ་ཡ་ཤ་ཡན་དྲིང།

14. ག་ཞིས་ཤུག་རྟུག་ས་ལི་ཧོ་ཡ་ཤ་ཡན་དྲིང།

15. ག་ཙོག་སེ་ཅང་གི་ས་ལི་ཧོ་ཡ་ཤ་ཡན་དྲིང།

16. ཀྱི་ཤུར་ལྷ་འབྲོག་ས་ལི་ཧོ་ཡ་ཤ་ཡན་དྲིང།

17. ཧ་ནུ་ཧན་དྲང་མིར་ས་ལི་ཧོ་ཡ་ཤ་ཡན་དྲིང།

18. ས་ཉིད་ས་ཚུག་ཞེད།

19. དུ་བོ་རོ་ད་རྩུ་ཉེ་སོ་དེ་ཅན།

20. ཧོ་ཧ་ཡོན་མ་སྙོན་མན་དེ་དེ་མན་དེ་མན་དེ་ཤིན།

21. རྡི་རྡོན་མལ་མལ།

22. མན་དེ་དེ་མན་དེ་ཤིན།

23. ཧོ་རྐྱ་ཀེ་ཡོན་མལ་མལ།

24. མན་དེ་དེ་མན་དེ་ཤིན།

25. ཧོ་ཀེ་ཡོན་མལ་མལ།།

XXXVII. The Azhaug, a Benefactor.

Dard Text.

1. སྦུ་རྡེན་ལྷ་རྡེན་སྦུལ་མོ།
2. ཧང་ཧང་དོ་དོ་ཧང་ཡེ་སྦུམ་མོ།
3. ཀར་ཙོལ་ཕོག་ཕེའ་གདགས་སེ།
4. ལྷ་ཡུལ་དུ་ཧེ་རས་སྦུ་ཤིག།

13. པར་ཀུན་ད་གནམ་དཀྱིལ་གྱི་ཁ་དྲང་ལ་འདུག།
གཞི་བདག་ལ་ཡ་ཤ།

14. ག་བེས་ནི་ཤུག་པ་མང་པོའི་རྩར་འདུག།

15. གནོག་ནི་ལྷ་ཡི་ལྷུང་མའི་རྩར་འདུག། གཞི་བདག་ལ་ཡ་ཤ།

16. སྨྲི་ཤུར་ལ་ལྷ་ཡི་འབྲོག། གཞི་བདག་ལ་ཡ་ཤ།

17. ཧན་དྲང་མེར་ཧ་ནུའི་འབྲོག། གཞི་བདག་ལ་ཡ་ཤ།

18. (ས་ཚོལ་ནས་ཡོང་སྟེ) ས་ནི་ལ་མགོ་འཛུག་མཁན་ཡིན།

19. འབྲོག་གཉིས་ན་ཁྲུག་སྟོང་བསོད་བདེ་ཅན་འདུག།

20. འོ་ན་ལྷ་མོ་ཡུལ་ལྷ་གཞི་བདག།

21. འདི་བོ་རྩེས་སའི་རྒྱལ་ས་ཡིན།

22. ཀྱེ་ཡུལ་ལྷ་གཞི་བདག།

23. བྲ་ག་འདི་ལྷ་སག་གི་ས་ཁྲད་ཡིན།

24. ཡུལ་ལྷ་གཞི་བདག།

25. འདི་བྲ་གུ་ཀུན་གྱི་ཁར་རྩེས་ས་ཡིན།།

XXXVII. The Azhang, a Benefactor.

Tibetan Translation.

1. ལྷ་དང་མི་ཚང་མ་འཛོམས་ཤིག།

2. འོ་ན་འོ་ན་དེ་ནས་འོ་ན་ལེ་ཨ་ཞང་།

3. ཀལ་ཅོར་ཕོག་དང་ཕེའ་ག་ཏབས།

4. ལྷ་ཡུལ་ལ་ཁྲིར་ཤིག།

5. ཧ་ཡོན་མ་སྒྲོན་ལ་ཀྱིན།

6. ཚས་བྲུ་ཀོར་ཀོར་ལ་བྲུར་དུམ་ལན་དྲང་ཧང་ལེ།

7. བྲུ་སྒྲོ་ཟུར་ཀྱིན་པད་མ་ཧང་ལེ་སྨུམ་མོ།

8. བྲུར་དུམ་ལན་དྲང་རོག་ལེད་ག་ཤན་སྨུམ་མོ།

9. ཨ་རག་སིལ་མ་ཀྱིལ་ལེད་ག་ཤན་སྨུམ་མོ།

10. ཨ་རག་དི་རིག་ཕིད་ལེད་ག་ཤན་སྨུམ་མོ།

11. གོན་ན་ཞུལ་ལི་གིན་ལེད་ག་ཤན་ལེ་སྨུམ་མོ།

12. ཚུ་ཕོ་ལག་ཚངས་བྲུ་དྲལ་ལེད་ག་ཤན་སྨུམ་མོ།

13. ད་ཙུ་ནེ་ན་ཚུང་སྦེར་ལེད་ག་ཤན་སྨུམ་མོ།

14. ཁྲོམ་ནང་ཆེན་མོ་གྲལ་ལེད་ག་ཤན་སྨུམ་མོ།

15. ཁྲུད་ཁྲེད་དོ་དོ་ཁྲེད་ནུ་སྨུམ་མོ།

XXXVIII. The Beautiful Girls of Da.

Dard Text.

1. ཙབ་ཙབ་དོ་དོ་ཨུ་ཐེད་ལེ་སྨུམ་མོ།

2. ཨ་སི་གོ་བོང་ལྦེམ་བ་ལེ་སྨུམ་མོ།

3. ཨ་སི་སྤྲ་ལོ་རྒྱལ་ལྦུང་ལེ་སྨུམ་མོ།

4. ཞག་གོར་ཧལ་ག་དྲུམ་དྲུམ་ལེ་སྨུམ་མོ།

5. ཨ་སི་ནོ་ལོ་ཉི་ཤར་ལེ་སྨུམ་མོ།

5. ང་དང་ཚང་ཀོད་དེ་རྩ་ཆ་ཡིན།

6. ཚམས་དེའི་ནང་ན་གསེར་ཡུ་རི་མེན་ཏོག་ཡོད་ལེ།

7. ཟུར་རྒྱན་མེན་ཏོག་པད་མ་ཡོད་ལེ་ཨ་ཞང་།

8. གསེར་ཡུ་རི་དང་ལན་དྲང་མདོག་བདེ་མོ་ཡོད་ལེ་ཨ་འང་།

9. ཨ་རག་སྲིང་མ་སྐྱིལ་དེ་བོར་མཁན་གྱི་ཨ་ཞང་།

10. ཨ་རག་སྲིབ་གཅིག་ལ་འཐུང་མཁན་གྱི་ཨ་ཞང་།

11. ཞོ་སྣུགས་ཟུམ་མཁན་གྱི་ཨ་ཞང་།

12. རྩུ་བོན་ཁྲིད་འཆང་བཏང་མཁན་གྱི་ཨ་ཞང་།

13. ཁྲོག་སྤོང་ན་རྩུང་བདེ་མོ་སྐྱུང་མཁན་གྱི་ཨ་ཞང་།

14. ཁྲིམ་ཆེན་པོ་ལ་གྲལ་བདེ་མོ་བཙོ་མཁན་གྱི་ཨ་ཞང་།

15. ཟོ་ཟོ་དེ་ནས་ཟོས་ཤིག་ཏེ་ཨ་ཞང་།།

XXXVIII. The Beautiful Girls of Da.

Tibetan Translation.

1. དུར་དུར་ལ་དེ་ནས་ལོངས་ཨ་ཞང་།

2. ང་ཧི་གཟུགས་པོ་བདེ་མོ་ཡོད་ཨ་ཞང་།

3. ང་ཧི་སྨ་ལོ་རྒྱ་ལྷུང་དང་འདྲ་ལེ་ཨ་ཞང་།

4. ལན་བུ་ནི་འོད་ཅན་དང་པོན་པོན་དང་འདྲ་ལེ་ཨ་ཞང་།

5. ང་ཧི་དཔལ་པ་ཉི་མ་དང་མཆོགས་ལེ་ཨ་ཞང་།

6. ཨ་སི་ཨ་བྲི་བྲིར་སིག་ལོ་སྨུམ་མོ།

7. ཨ་སི་མིག་སྨྲ་ཆོ་ལྷིངས་ལོ་སྨུམ་མོ།

8. ཨ་སི་ནམ་ཆ་སེར་ཙ་དོར་ཕང་ལོ་སྨུམ་མོ།

9. ཨ་སི་དན་ནི་སྨུན་དྲ་ལོ་སྨུམ་མོ།

10. ཨ་སི་རྒུམ་པོ་པོར་ཙོས་ལོ་སྨུམ་མོ།

11. ཨ་སི་མལ་མལ་འཛོམ་པོ་ལོ་སྨུམ་མོ།

12. ལུ་བལ་ལུབ་བྲུག་གུ་ལུས་སྨྱོའི་ཆ་ལོ་སྨུམ་མོ།

13. ཨུ་སོད་སྲོལ་ལོ་སྨྱོའི་ཆ་ལོ་སྨུམ་མོ།

14. ཙ་དར་སྲོལ་ལོ་སྨྱོའི་ཆ་ལོ་སྨུམ་མོ།

15. སྨུ་སོ་སྲོལ་ལོ་སྨྱོའི་ཆ་ལོ་སྨུམ་མོ།

16. ཏོ་ཏོ་སྲིམ་སྲིམ་སྲིམ་སྲིམ།།

XXXIX. General Love.

Dard Text.

1. ལོ་རྗོ་མོ་རྗོ་གྲ་ཞམ།

2. ནང་གོང་སྨུ་རྫུ་རྫུ་མེ་ལིག་དེ།

3. རྡིང་པག་གོར་ཁད་དི་བྲུ་འི་སྲིམ་སྲིམ་སྲིམ།

4. ཏང་སེ་ཏོ་ཏོ་ལོ་ཏང་སེ།

5. ནང་གོང་སྨུ་ཏི་བྲུ་འི།

6. ང་དེ་མིག་པོ་གཟི་མིག་ཡོད་ལི་ཨ་ཞང།

7. ང་དེ་མིག་སྨ་ལང་སྟེ་ཡོད་ལི་ཨ་ཞང།

8. ང་དེ་ཏྲ་ཚ་ཤོལ་ཤོལ་ཡོད་ལི་ཨ་ཞང།

9. ང་དེ་སོ་པོ་སྤུ་རིག་འདྲ་ཡོད་ལི་ཨ་ཞང།

10. ང་དེ་ཁམ་རྩ་པོག་པོག་ཡོད་ཨ་ཞང་ལི།

11. ང་དེ་སྐྱེས་པའི་ཕ་ཡུལ་འཛོམ་སྟེ་ཡོད་ལི་ཨ་ཞང།

12. ལུག་པལ་ལི་གོན་ཅེས་སྤྲོས་ཤིག་ལི་ཨ་ཞང།

13. བོད་རྒྱལ་ལ་སྤྲོས་ལི་ཨ་ཞང།

14. ཙ་དར་རྒྱལ་ལ་སྤྲོས་ལི་ཨ་ཞང།

15. མིན་དོག་རྒྱལ་ལ་སྤྲོས་འདང་ལི་ཨ་ཞང།

16. དེ་ནས་ཁྲིམ་ཁྲིམ་ཁྲིམ།།

XXXIX. General Love.

Tibetan Translation.

1. དེ་ནས་ཁྱོད་རང་གིས་ང་ལ་ཡ་ཤ་ཅེས།

2. བུར་ལ་ཡུལ་ལ་སྟོས།

3. སྟོན་པའི་སྤང་ཟ་མཁན་གྱི་བུ། ཁྲིམ་ཁྲིམ་ཁྲིམ།

4. ཁྱོད་ཀྱིས་ང་ལ་ཡ་ཤ་བཅོ་དགོས།

5. ཡུལ་ལ་ཉལ་མཁན་གྱི་བུ་མོ།

6. ཚམ་་མ་ཀྵམ་་ཀྵམ།

7. ནང་་གོང་དོ་དོ་ལི་་ཡོན་བྲུན་་། ཡོ་་དོ་མོ་་དོ་གྲ་་ཞེ་ན།

8. ཀྲི་་ཤུར་དོ་དོ་སྨུའི་་ཞུན་བན་་།

9. སྐྱིད་་ས་དོ་དོ་ཕ་་ཡུལ་བེད་་།

10. ཡོ་་དོ་མོ་་དོ་གྲ་་ཞེ་མ།

11. ནང་་གོང་ཙུ་ཡང་་མ་པླུ་་ཚུང་།

12. བར་་ཚམ་སྲུ་ཙུ་སེར་་མོ་པླུ་་ཚུང་།

13. ཡལ་་དོར་ཙུ་ཡང་་དཀར་པླུ་་ཚུང་།

14. ཀྲི་་ཤུར་ཙུ་དོ་་དོ་ཀྲུ་་ཀྲིན་ཡང་་མ་པླུ་་ཚུང་།

15. སྐྱིད་་བོ་བེང་་བེང་བེད་་།

16. རིཛ་་ན་མོ་ལེ་ཁོ་དྲུ་་།

17. ཡེ་་སདུ་བྲུས་་སིག་ཐེ་་།

18. ཡ་་ཤ་དོ་་དོ་ཀ་་དིག་ཐེ་་།།

XL. Dawn of Morning.

Dard Text.

1. བེང་་སེ་པ་་ཡི་ས་དྲིན་་།

2. ཡུས་་ཡུང་དོ་ཡུས་་ཡུང་དོ།

3. སུམ་་མོ་དོ་དོ་དུ་ཡླ་་ཀི་་ཡུང་།

6. ཚམ་མ་ཚམ་ཚམ།

7. རས་དན་ཡུལ་ལྷ་ཅིའི་ཡུལ།

8. ཀྱི་ཤུར་འབྲོག་པི་ཅིའི་ཡུལ།

9. སྐྱིད་པོ་ཡོད་མཁན་ཚང་མ་ང་རང་གི་ཕ་ཡུལ།

10. དེ་ནས་ང་ལ་གཅིས་པ་ཅོས།

11. ཡུལ་ལ་ཡང་མ་འཚོས་སེད།

12. བར་ལ་གསེར་མོ་སྨིན་ནེད།

13. ཡང་དོར་ཡང་དཀར་སྨིན་ནེད།

14. ཀྱི་ཤུར་ལ་སྨན་མ་སྨིན་ནེད།

15. སྐྱིད་པོ་ང་དང་ལ་ཡིན་ནོག།

16. ཉི་རང་ལ་ཞུ་དཀོན་མཆོག།

17. ཡ་དོ་ང་ལ་ཙ་ཐིག་ཅིག་སྐྱུལ།

18. ཡ་ཤ་ཟེར་དེ་ལག་པ་སྐོར།།

XL. Dawn of Morning.

Tibetan Translation.

1. ང་དང་ངེས་དེ་ཙུ་ལུག་བསམ་ཡིན།

2. གནམ་ལངས་སེད། གནམ་ལངས་སེད།

3. ཨ་ཞང་ལ་དེ་ནས་གླང་མོ་ཡོང་འདུག།

4. སྦྲར་ཕྲེ་དོ་མི་ནྭ་རོ་སྣྭ་ཀོ་འིགར་ཛུང་ནྭ་ལོ་འོ་བྲ་འི།
5. ལུས་ཡུང་དོ་སྨུམ་མོ་དོ་དོ་ཉ་ཀི་ཡུང་།
6. སྨུམ་མོས་དོ་དོ་ལབ་ཐིག་དེ་ཟུང་།
7. སྨུམ་མོས་སེ་དོ་ཕུབ་ཐིག་ཕུང་།
8. ལུས་ཡུང་དོ་སྨུམ་མོ་དོ་བྲ་མི་ཡ་ཡུང་།
9. སྨུམ་མོས་སེ་དོ་ལ་དིག་དེ་ཟུང་།
10. ལུས་ཡུང་དོ་སྨུམ་མོ་ཤྲུ་མིའོ་ཡུང་།
11. ཞེལ་དང་དོ་སྨུམ་མོ་སྲུང་།
12. སྐྱི་ར་རུ་བར་ཁྱད་སྣྭ་ཡུང་།
13. ཚོའིལ་དོ་ནམ་ལང་སེ་དོ་ཨུ་ཕྲེ་ཟུང་།།

XLI. Pastoral Song.

Dard Text.

1. ཚོའིལ་དོ་སྨུམ་མོ་པའི་དྲི་གྲུང་།
2. རྫ་མ་བོ་མོ་རིག་ཕྲེ་ལོ་སྨུམ་མོ།
3. སྨུམ་མོ་ཕྲུན་ཧིད་ལ་སྐྱེ།
4. ཞེ་ལི་དོ་མེ་རིག་གྲོ་བའི་ལོ་སྨུམ་མོ།
5. སྨུམ་མོ་སེ་དོ་པ་ཨི་དོ་ལྦར་པེ་རེ་དོ་ཡེ།
6. ཡལ་དོར་ཞུང་སྲུ་རུ་དེ་ལོ་སྨུམ་མོ།
7. དི་ལི་འུ་དེལ་མར་ཕང་ལོ་སྨུམ་མོ།
8. ཕལ་དྲུ་རོ་སྤང་ཚོ་ཕང་ལོ་སྨུམ་མོ།

4. གྲང་གྲང་ཅིག་བཅོ་རྡུག་འབྲོག་པས་ཅི་ཟེར་འདུག་ལེ།
5. གནམ་ལང་སྐྱེ་ཨ་ཞང་ལ་སྐོམ་སྐྱེ་ཡོང་ངེད།
6. ཨ་ཞང་ངེས་མི་སླབ་ཅིག་བཅོ་ཡིན།
7. ཨ་ཞང་ངེས་ཇུབ་ཅིག་བཅོ་ཡིན།
8. གནམ་ལང་སྐྱེ་ཨ་ཞང་ལྷོགས་སེད།
9. ཨ་ཞང་ངེས་ཕོ་ཇབ་ཅིག་བཅོ་ཡིན།
10. གནམ་ལང་སྐྱེ་ཨ་ཞང་ངལ་ལེད།
11. ཕི་སྒྲོག་ཨ་ཞང་གཉིད་ལོག་གེད།
12. གཉིད་ལ་སྨིན་བརླབས་ཡོང་ཡིན།
13. སྤུ་མོ་གནམ་ལང་སྐྱེ་ཨ་ཞང་ལངས་སེད།།

XLI. Pastoral Song.

Tibetan Translation.

1. སྤུ་མོ་ཨ་ཞང་ར་རྫི་ལ་ཆེན།
2. ཟླ་ཅེས་ཞིམ་པོ་ཞིག་ཅོས་ཨ་ཞང་ལེ།
3. ཨ་ཞང་འགྲངས་འདུག་ག་སྟོས།
4. ཛ་ར་ཞིམ་པོ་ཞིག་འཁུར་དེ་སོང་ལེ་ཨ་ཞང་།
5. ཨ་ཞང་ངེས་ར་ལུག་གི་གྲོད་པ་བཀང་སྐྱེ་ཁྱོང་།
6. ཡལ་རྫོར་གཞུང་ལ་སོང་།
7. ཚས་སྒྲིས་མེན་དོག་ཡོད་ལེ་ཨ་ཞང་།
8. གསེར་པོའི་སྦྲང་རྩི་ཡོད།

9. སབ་ཟང་ཁ་གོལ་ཧང་ལེོ་སྨུམ་མོ།

10. ཛམ་ཚོ་བ་ཧ་ས་ཧང་ལེོ་སྨུམ་མོ།

11. ཞེལ་རང་ཉུབ་པད་ལེོ་སྨུམ་མོ།

12. པའི་ལྦར་པེ་རེད་ལེོ་སྨུམ་མོ།

13. དི་ཛ་ན་མོ་ལེོ་སྨུམ་མོ།

14. སྦུ་ཙུ་ཁཤཧྲུ་རི་ལེོ་སྨུམ་མོ༎

XLII. The Blessed Herdsman.

Dard Text.

1. ཨོ་ཨོ་དུད་ཕེད་ལེོ་སྨུམ་མོ།

2. ཁོ་དྲ་རེ་ཞུ་ཞེད་ལེོ་སྨུམ་མོ།

3. ལུས་ཡུང་དོ་ལུས་ཡུང་དོ་ཀྲ་ལི་དུད།

4. སྦུ་སྦུན་ལེོ་སྨུམ་མོ།

5. དུད་ཕུན་ཛོལ་ལེོ་སྨུམ་མོ།

XLIII. Preparation of Curdled Milk.

Dard Text.

1. ཙོའལ་དོ་ལུས་ཡུང་དོ་ལེོ་སྨུམ་མོ།

2. སྦུ་ཙ་སྐྱི་ཕུང་དོ་ཀྲ་ཨི་སྟོ་ནེ་ཞེད་ལེོ་སྨུམ་མོ།

3. ཀྲ་ཨི་ནགལེ་ཙུན་ལེོ་སྨུམ་མོ།

9. རྟ་བཟང་ཡོད་ལེ་ཨ་ཞང།

10. འཚོ་བ་འཛམ་པོ་དང་ལེགས་མོ་ཡོད།

11. ཕྱི་ཕྲོག་ཡོངས་སེད་ལེ་ཨ་ཞང།

12. ར་ལུག་གི་གྲོད་པ་འགྲངས་དོག་ལེ་ཨ་ཞང།

13. ཉེ་རང་ལ་ཕྱུ་ཨ་ཞང།

14. བདང་ར་ལ་བཀགགས་དོང་ལེ་ཨ་ཞང།།

XLII. The Blessed Herdsman.

Tibetan Translation.

1. ར་མས་འོ་མ་བདང་ངེད་ལེ་ཨ་ཞང།

2. དཀོན་མཆོག་ལ་ཞུ་རི་ན་འདུག་ལེ་ཨ་ཞང།

3. གནམ་ལང་སྦྱེ་རི་གུ་སྐྱེས།

4. བདང་ར་གང་སོང་ལེ་ཨ་ཞང།

5. འོ་མ་སྣང་ཤིག་ལེ་ཨ་ཞང།།

XLIII. Preparation of Curdled Milk.

Tibetan Translation.

1. སྤུ་ཕྲོག་ལངས་འདུག་ལེ་ཨ་ཞང།།

2. བདང་ར་ལ་ལྷུ་ན་རི་གུ་དང་གང་སྟེ་ཡོད་ལེ་ཨ་ཞང།

3. རི་གུ་ཕྱིང་ཤིག་ལེ་ཨ་ཞང།

4. ཀྐ་ལི་པག་ཀོར་བྲུན་ལོ་སྒུམ་མོ།

5. ཀྐ་ལི་སེ་ཚ་རག་ཨ་རི་འེན་ནེ་ལོ་སྒུམ་མོ།

6. ཚ་ལིན་དྲ་དུད་ཚིན་ཉུན་ལོ་སྒུམ་མོ།

7. པོ་དོ་དུད་སྦྲ་ཏུན་ལོ་སྒུམ་མོ།

8. ཀན་ཏ་པ་ཡུན་ལོ་སྒུམ་མོ།

9. ཀན་སྦྲོལ་ལོ་བེད་ལོ་སྒུམ་མོ།

10. པོ་དོ་ཀན་ནས་ཕོག་དྲུ་ལོ་སྒུམ་མོ།

11. ཀན་ནས་འུ་སྤྲི་སང་ལི་འུན་ལོ་སྒུམ་མོ།

12. པོ་དོ་ཨུ་ཐྲི་དེ་ལོ་སྒུམ་མོ།

13. བྲུན་ཧྲུང་ཁྲོར་ཁྲོར་ལོ་སྒུམ་མོ།

14. བྲ་རིང་ཉེར་རྩུ་བེ་ཡ་སྒུན་ལོ་སྒུམ་མོ།

XLIV. Profits of Pasture-life.

Dard Text.

1. པོ་དོམ་སམ་ནི་ཀ་ལོ་སྒུམ་མོ།

2. པོ་དོ་གྷི་གྲོ་ར་བེད་ལོ་སྒུམ་མོ།

3. སྒོད་རི་ཕུ་ཨིག་ཐེད་ལོ་སྒུམ་མོ།

4. ར་ཉི་སེ་པག་ཀོར་བྲུན་ལོ་སྒུམ་མོ།

5. ཡླ་ཕ་ཏོ་ཁབ་ཁབ་བེད་ལོ་སྒུམ་མོ།

4. རི་གུ་དང་སྤྲང་གང་སྟེ་ཡོད་ལེ་ཨ་ཞང།

5. རི་གུ་ཀུན་གྱིས་ཚང་རག་བདང་ངེད་ལེ་ཨ་ཞང།

6. རི་གུ་ལ་འོ་མ་བཙན་རེད་ཨ་ཞང།

7. དེ་ནས་འོ་མ་བཙོར་འང་ལེ་ཨ་ཞང།

8. ཞོ་བསྲོ་སྟེ་སྐོལ་འང་ལེ་ཨ་ཞང།

9. ཞོ་ གྲུལ་ལ་སོང་དོག་ལེ་ཨ་ཞང།

10. དེ་ནས་ཞོ་ལ་ཡོག་དོང་ལེ་ཨ་ཞང།

11. ཞོ་ནས་འོ་སྨྲི་འཐེན་དོང་ལེ་ཨ་ཞང།

12. དེ་ནས་ཁ་ལ་ཏུབ་གཅིག་དོང་ལེ་ཨ་ཞང།

13. འགྲང་འགྲངས་ཚུག་པ་ཟེ་ལེ་ཨ་ཞང།

14. ཚང་རྐྱལ་པའི་ནང་ལ་སླུགས་དོང་ལེ་ཨ་ཞང།

XLIV. Profits of Pasture-life.

Tibetan Translation.

1. དེ་ནས་ངས་མར་སྒྲོག་འདུག་ལེ་ཨ་ཞང།

2. དེ་ནས་ངས་མར་བཙག་འདུག་ལེ་ཨ་ཞང།

3. དཀོན་མཆོག་ལ་ཕུ་བ་ཞིག་ཕུལ་འདུག་ལེ་ཨ་ཞང།

4. ལུག་གུ་དང་སྤྲང་གང་སྟེ་ཡོད་ལེ་ཨ་ཞང།

5. བལ་བོང་བོང་འཕེལ་འདུག་ལེ་ཨ་ཞང།

6. སྒྲིང་་ངེ་ཊོ་ཀིར་་ཡི་ཞེད་་ལྀོ་སྨུམ་་མོ།

7. མིང་ངར་་རྀ་མར་་རེ་ཤོན་་ལྀོ་སྨུམ་་མོ།

8. ཀྲུར་་ལྀོ་མར་་རེ་ཤོན་་ལྀོ་སྨུམ་་མོ།

Notes.

This hymnal (Nos. XXXI-XLIV) is sung at Da, Garkunu, and the other villages of the Eastern Dards (Shina) at the time of the Bŏno-nā festival, which is celebrated every third year. It was celebrated in 1903, and will be celebrated again in 1906. The above songs were dictated by *'aBrug bkrashis*, who is a *lha bab* and one of the principal recitors at the festival. Being a *lha bab*, *i.e.*, a person, on whom the gods descend, or who becomes possessed by their spirits, he officiates as a priest at sheep-offerings and other rites of their Pre-Buddhist religion. The songs were written down and furnished with a West-Tibetan translation by *Tharrnyed chos 'aphel*, who is now a Christian Catechist, but who used to be a Buddhist lama at Da and Garkunu, about seven years ago. Although he understands the language of the Eastern Dards perfectly well, the Tibetan alphabet presented great difficulties, when applied to the foreign sounds of an Aryan language. But on the whole the orthography is tolerably accurate. Accentuated syllables are marked by two dots (*thseg*). I hope to edit the same songs once more with Roman transscription and a full vocabulary of all the words and forms occuring in the hymnal. The songs are called the 18 songs (*glu athrungsh*); but at present there appear to be only 14 of them. I suppose that in several cases (see for instance No XXXVII) several originally separate songs grew together and afterwards were taken for one single song. The word *mummo*, which signifies uncle at the present day (the ordinary term of address to male persons), is said to stand for 'uncle of the past' in the songs. Therefore it has to be translated by 'fore-father.' But in songs Nos. XLII-XLIV, the *mummo* seems to be the male Dard of the present day.

The hymnal is interesting for two reasons: (1) it contains the last remnants of Dard mythology, particularly their account of the origin of the world. The system of colours as contained in it reminds us of the Tibetan *g Ling chos*. (2) it contains the historical recollections of the Eastern Dards (compare No. XXXVI). They have not yet forgotten that at one time their forefathers emigrated from Gilgit, and the list of place-names shows the route of their spreading towards south-east, up the Indus-valley very well. All the villages, mentioned in the songs, are well-known places. If

6. ཏུ་ཙོ་འཁྲིལ་ལིན་འདུག་ལེ་ཨ་ཞང།

7. ཐོ་ལགས་བསད་དེ་ཟ་ཡིན་ལེ་ཨ་ཞང།

8. སྐམ་པོ་ལགས་བསད་དེ་ཟ་ཡིན་ལེ་ཨ་ཞང།།

Notes.

Abstract of contents. No. XXXI. Preparations for the festival. All the provisions and flowers, required for the festival, are ordered to be brought.

No. XXXII. Account of the origin of the world. Out of the water a meadow rose, and three mountains grew on that meadow. The names of the mountains are: The white, the red and the blue jewel-hill. On these three hills three trees grew. Their names are: The white, the blue and the red sandal-tree. Three birds grew on the three trees. Their names are: The wild eagle (on the white tree), the fowl (on the red tree), and the black *Biru jolmo* on the blue tree. [The three mountains and trees are probably thought to exist one on the top of the other, and thus to constitute the three worlds. Compare the mythology of the *g Ling chos*].

No. XXXIII. Description of a festival at Gilgit, the home of the fore-fathers of the Eastern Dards. The boys of Gilgit and Brushal, and the girls of Rashtran and Sathsil, were assembled for a dance, with the lion-king of Gilgit at the head of the dancers. Suddenly a noise was heard on the Ambiri-hill, and a herd of ibex discovered. It is described in full, how these ibex were hunted with bow and arrow, and how the meat was distributed.

No. XXXIII. Description of a festival at Gilgit, the home of the fore-fathers of the Eastern Dards. The boys of Gilgit and Brushal, and the girls of Rashtran and Sathil, were assembled for a dance, with the lion-king of Gilgit at the head of the dancers. Suddenly a noise was heard on the Ambiri-hill, and a herd of ibex discovered. It is described in full, how these ibex were hunted with bow and arrow, and how the meat was distributed.

No. XXXIV. The happy hunter is placed at the head of the dancers, carrying the horn, the skin etc. of the ibex. When he has finished dancing, he is ordered to walk towards east.

No. XXXV. The question is asked, from whence the gods (*yandring*) come. It is answered that they come out of the middle of the sky. Therefore everybody puts on his best suit. [The gods are supposed to be present at the dance].

No. XXXVI. The emigration from Gilgit. The Dards went to *Rong churgyud*, thence to *Gusur* and *Koarto kumar*, both famous for their currants; thence to *Skardogod*, famous for willows; thence they cannot be found on maps, it is due to the terrible orthography of Indian maps.

As regards the language of the songs, it is a very mixed language. Not only are about half of the words either pure Tibetan or derived from Tibetan stems, but also the grammatical system has been adapted to a far degree to that of the Tibetan language. I think I shall not be blamed for having included the Dard hymnal in my collection of Ladakhi songs. It has been the Ladakhi dialect which has influenced the language of the Minaro-Dards (as they call themselves), and the Dard villages have been part of the Ladakhi kingdom for several centuries.

Pronunciation of the Dard texts: All letters are to be pronounced in full; for instance *byun* not to be pronounced *jun*, but *byun*; *gra* not *dra*, but *gra*. The gutturals *kh* and *gh* are denoted by Tibetan *rkh* and *rg*. German ö is expressed by o + e; slavonic ou is expressed by o. + u.

XLV. Song of the Bunan Pilgrim.

1. དཀོན་མཆོག་མཁྱེན།
2. དེ་དུས་ཕྱི་དྲིག་ཀྱི་ར་རེ་གྲུན།
3. བཀྲ་ཤིས་པར་གྲུར་དེ་གྲུན།
4. དཀོན་མཆོག་མཁྱེན།།

XLVI. Song of the Bunan Pilgrim.

1. འཕགས་པ་མཁྱེན།

to *Shiggar* or *Chambrozhing*; thence to *Kyeris chumghag*, and *Ghasing mantrokhar*, famous for gravel; thence to *Parkudda*, exactly under the middle of the sky; thence to *Gabis*, famous for pencil-cedars, thence to *Ganog*, famous on account of its holy willow-tree; thence to *Kyishur*, the field of the gods (*lha*); thence to *Handrangmir* and *Haun*. When coming from *Sa theil* (near Gilgit), *Sanid* was founded first of all.

No. XXXVII. An offering is ordered to be brought to the country of the gods (*lha yul*). We shall all go there! Then the fore-father (*mummo*) is praised as the benefactor of the people.

No. XXXVIII. The girls rise, praising their own beauty and attractions, and admonish the boys (or ancestors?) to decorate their own persons afresh and join the dance.

No. XXXIX. The good harvest in the different villages is praised. In between the cry, to show love (probably sensual love) occurs.

No. XL. The first light of the morning appears (the festival lasts during the whole of the night). The fore-father feels cold, hungry, thirsty and tired. He is cared for.

No. XLI. The fore-father, provided with some food, takes the goats and sheep to the pasture-ground; in the evening he brings the herds home with their stomachs filled.

No. XLII. The goats are milked; [next] morning a kid is born.

No. XLIII. A shepherd-scene. Curdled milk is made and eaten.

No. XLIV. Butter is made; the sheep are thriving; the fattest rams and geldings will be killed and eaten.

XLV. Song of the Bunan Pilgrim.

1. O God,

2. Something pure, oh may it appear!

3. Some happines, oh may it come to pass!

4. O God.

XLVI. Song of the Bunan Pilgrim.

1. O exalted one,

2. ཚེ་ཚེ་དིག་ཀྱི་སྐྱུ་རེ་ད།

3. དྲུན་གྱིས་ཕྲུགས་ཞེ་ལེ་འ།

4. དྲུན་དོག་རྒྱུམ་ཚོད་དིག་ཀྱི་ཕྱུལ་ཅིག།

5. འཕགས་པ་མཁྱེན།།

XLVII. Song of the Bunan Pilgrim.

1. དཀོན་མཆོག་མཁྱེན།

2. སྐྲོག་དོག་ར་རེ་ཐད།

3. གྲུམ་དོག་ལེབ་ཀ་ཙ་ཨ་སྒྲོག།

4. དམ་ཤི་དིག་ཀྱི་ར་རེ་ད་ཙ་གྲུན།

5. དཀོན་མཆོག་མཁྱེན།།

XLVIII. Song of the Bunan Pilgrim.

1. འཕགས་པ་མཁྱེན།

2. ནད་ར་རེ་ཐད།

3. ཧྱིན་ཇོག་སྐྱབས་མིག་ཅི།

4. ཡོག་ཙ་གྲུན།

5. ང་རོ་ཕི་རོ་དྲུན་དེན་ཞི་པ་ཡེན།

6. ཁྲི་རིག་ཚུག་ཚོ་རོག།

7. ཁའི་ཨ་ཙོ་ཁྲུག་ཙུམ་ནི་ལ།

8. ཐ་ཧྲུ་ཨེ་པོ་དིག་ཀྱི་ར་རེ་གྲུན།

9. འཕགས་པ་མཁྱེན།།

2. Something kind, oh may it be granted!

3. Mayest thou show us mercy!

4. We shall give thee a great offering,

5. O exalted one!

XLVII. Song of the Bunan Pilgrim.

1. O God,

2. Do not let my life be endangered,

3. Until [I] arrive home again!

4. Something pure, oh may it be granted,

5. O God!

XLVIII. Song of the Bunan Pilgrim.

1. O exalted one!

2. Let no illness come!

3. Render us salvation!

4. Mayest thou think of it!

5. Morning and evening we trust in thee!

6. Later on in life,

7. Whatever [sort of] way I may find,

8. Oh, mayest thou grant [there] something good!

9. O exalted one!

Notes.

I think, I shall not be blamed for having incorporated a few Bunan songs in my collection of Ladakhi songs. Several centuries ago, Lahoul was a province of the Ladakhi kingdom, and up to the present, the dialect of Eastern Ladakh has influenced the Bunan language. Many Tibetan words have entered the Bunan language at a time when their pronunciation was fuller than at the present day (compare Jäschke, JASB, Vol. XXXIV). Such a word we have in XLVII, 2; *strog* represents a very ancient type of pronunciation of the word *srog*. Compare Lad. Grammar, laws of sound, No. 2.

XLIX. The poor Girl and the rich Girl.

P. 1. ཁྲེད་ནི་ཕྱུག་པོའི་ཕྱུག་ཕྲུག།
དཀར་ཡོལ་ནང་ལ་འོ་མ།
ང་ནི་མེད་པའི་མེད་ཕྲུག།
ཐོར་པ་ནང་ལ་དར་བ།
ཁྲེད་ནི་ཕྱུག་པོའི་ཕྱུག་ཕྲུག།
གོས་ཆེན་ས་ལ་སྐྱིལ་སོང་།
ང་ནི་མེད་པའི་མེད་ཕྲུག།
བེམ་པོ་ས་ལ་སྐྱིལ་སོང་།།

R. 2. རྒྱུ་ཞིག་འཕྲུང་ཡིན་བསམ་སྟེ།
ལུངས་པོའི་མཐའ་མར་བསྐྱེབ་སོང་།
རྒྱུ་ནི་ཁྲུགས་ཀྱིས་བསྐམས་སོང་།
རྒྱུ་ནི་འཕྲུང་ངོ་མ་རྟོགས།
ཉ་མོ་ཁྲུགས་ཀྱིས་བསྐམས་སོང་།
ངང་པའི་གློ་ཐག་ཆོད་སོང་།།

Notes.

The Bunan pilgrim songs which constitute the bulk of Bunan native literature, are sung on pilgrimages of the Bunan people to Triloknath. Although all those songs which Rev. A. W. Heyde has collected (the above four were taken from his collection) are very short, they last the pilgrims a long way, on account of endless repetitions.

XLIX. The poor Girl and the rich Girl.

P. 1. Oh, you rich child of a rich man,
You have milk [poured] in china.
I, the poor child of one who possesses nothing,
I have [only] buttermilk [poured] in a cup.
Oh, you rich child of a rich man,
Your silk dress touches the ground
I am the poor child of one who possesses nothing,
And my rags touch the ground.

R. 2. Thinking, I will drink some water,
I arrived at the bank of the river.
The water, however, was frozen,
And I did not get drinking water.
The fish was frozen in the ice,
And the hope of the duck was not fulfilled.

P. 3. ཨ་ཆེ་ཕྱུག་པོའི་མཐའ་མས།
པང་ལ་ཕྲུ་གུ་འཁྱེར་སོང་།
བྱང་པ་ཕྱུག་པོའི་མཐའ་མས
པང་ལ་ཕྲུ་གུ་འཁྱེར་སོང་།
ང་ནི་མེད་པའི་མེད་ཕྲུག།
པང་ལ་བི་ཕྲུག་འཁྱེར་སོང་།
ཁྱེད་ནི་ཕྱུག་པོའི་མཐའ་མས།
ཛ་ལ་གུར་གུར་བདང་སོང་།
ང་ནི་མེད་པའི་མེད་ཕྲུག།
ཆུ་ལ་གུར་གུར་བཏང་སོང་།།

R. 4. སྐྱིད་ཡིན་རྒྱགས་ཡིན་བསམ་སྟེ།
ལུག་གུ་སྤྱང་ལ་རྒྱབ་སོང་།
སྤྱང་ཀུ་ཡོང་ཡིན་བསམ་སྟེ།
སེམས་པོའི་ཡིད་ལ་མ་བསམ།།

Notes.

'*rnyilces*, when used of clothes, denotes 'touching the ground with the margin'; *blothag*, means 'hope'; *byangpa*, a man from *Byang thang*, North-East Ladakh.

L. The Tibetan Fiddle.

1. གྲམ་སྙན་ཆོ་བཀྲ་ཤིས་དབང་རྒྱལ་ལ།
ཡབ་ཆེན་མི་འདུག་མ་བསམ།

P. 3. Oh, you daughter-in-law of a rich man,
You carried a child on your lap.
Oh, you daughter-in law of a rich Northerner,
You carried a child on your lap.
I, the poor child of one who possesses nothing,
I carried a young cat on my lap.
Oh, you daughter-in-law of a rich man,
You stirred tea in the churn.
I, the poor child of one who possesses nothing
Had to stir water in the churn.

R 4. Thinking, it will become happy and fat,
They sent the lamb to the meadow.
The thought, that the wolf would come,
That thought did not enter their minds.

Notes.

The general idea is, that apparent happiness is not always real happiness. The parents, seeking their daughter's happiness, had married her to a rich man, without ever thinking of the wolf (the mother-in-law?).

L. The Tibetan Fiddle.

1. Do not think that my fiddle, called *bkrashis dbang rgyal*,
Does not possess a great father!

ཤིང་དེ་ནི་ལྷ་ཤིང་ཤུག་པ་ནི།
ཡབ་ཆེན་མེན་ནས་ཅི་ཡིན།།

2. གྲམ་སྙན་ཚོ་བཀྲ་ཤིས་དབང་རྒྱལ་ལ།
ཡུམ་ཆུང་མི་འདུག་མ་བསམ།
ཙོ་ཙོ་ལ་ར་མའི་གཙོར་སྐུད་པོ།
ཡུམ་ཆུང་མན་ནས་ཅི་ཡིན།།

3. གྲམ་སྙན་ཚོ་བཀྲ་ཤིས་དབང་རྒྱལ་ལ།
ཕོ་ནོ་མི་འདུག་མ་བསམ།
ལག་པའི་དྲན་མོ་བཅུ་ཀ་དེ་ནི།
ཕོ་ནོ་མན་ནས་ཅི་ཡིན།།

4. གྲམ་སྙན་ཚོབ་ཀྲ་ཤིས་དབང་རྒྱལ་ལ།
གཉེན་དྲུང་མི་འདུག་མ་བསམ།
རང་གི་ལ་ཞལ་གྱི་གསུངས་སྐད་དེ་
གཉེན་དྲུང་མན་ནས་ཅི་ཡིན།།

Refrain: ཤབ་ཤབ་མ་ཞིག་ཤབ་ཤབ་མཞིག།
ཚོ་སང་མ་ཞིག་སང་མོལ།།

Notes.

gram snyan, is probably the same as *sgra snyan*, guitar or violin; *thso* I cannot explain; *bkrashis dbang rgyal* means 'Happiness,... powerful king'; *tse tse*, a name of goats; *la* I can not explain; *ytsir skud*, strings of a violin; *pho no*, = *phubo nubo*, elder and younger brothers; *dranmo*, finger; *la zhal*, mouth.

If the divine wood of the pencil-cedar
Is not its great father, what else?

2. Do not think that my fiddle, called *bkrashis dbang royal,*
Does not possess a little mother!
If the strings from the goat
Are not its little mother, what else?

3. Do not think that my fiddle, called *bkrashis dbang rgyal,*
Does not possess any brothers!
If the ten fingers of my hand
Are not its brothers, what else?

4. Do not think that my fiddle called *bkrashis dbang rgyal!*
Does not possess any friends!
If the sweet sounds of its own mouth
Are not its friends, what else?

rain: Shab sháb ma zhíg shab sháb ma zhíg
Thse sáng ma zhíg sang mól.

Notes.

[1] This song is one of the few Tibetan songs, the metre *of which* is composed of jambs.

In editing the fourth and fifth series of Ladakhi songs my edition of these songs comes to an end. I find it impossible to spend any more of my private means in an enterprise which does not pay in the least.

A. H. Francke,
Khalatse, 2. IX. 03.

www.ingramcontent.com/pod-product-compliance
Lightning Source LLC
Chambersburg PA
CBHW030622270326
41927CB00007B/1284

* 9 7 8 3 3 3 7 3 8 4 7 4 6 *